Grace DeVito

ROADS TO THE WEST

Senior Authors

Roger C. Farr

Dorothy S. Strickland

Authors

Richard F. Abrahamson ♦ Alma Flor Ada ♦ Barbara Bowen Coulter

Bernice E. Cullinan ♦ Margaret A. Gallego

W. Dorsey Hammond

Nancy Roser ♦ Junko Yokota ♦ Hallie Kay Yopp

Senior Consultant

Asa G. Hilliard III

Consultants

Kanani Choy ♦ Lee Bennett Hopkins ♦ Stephen Krashen ♦ Rosalia Salinas

Harcourt Brace & Company

Orlando Atlanta Austin Boston San Francisco Chicago Dallas New York Toronto London

Copyright © 1997 by Harcourt Brace & Company. All rights reserved. ISBN 0-15-308336-0

1 2 3 4 5 6 7 8 9 10   048   99 98 97 96

ROADS TO THE WEST

CONTENTS

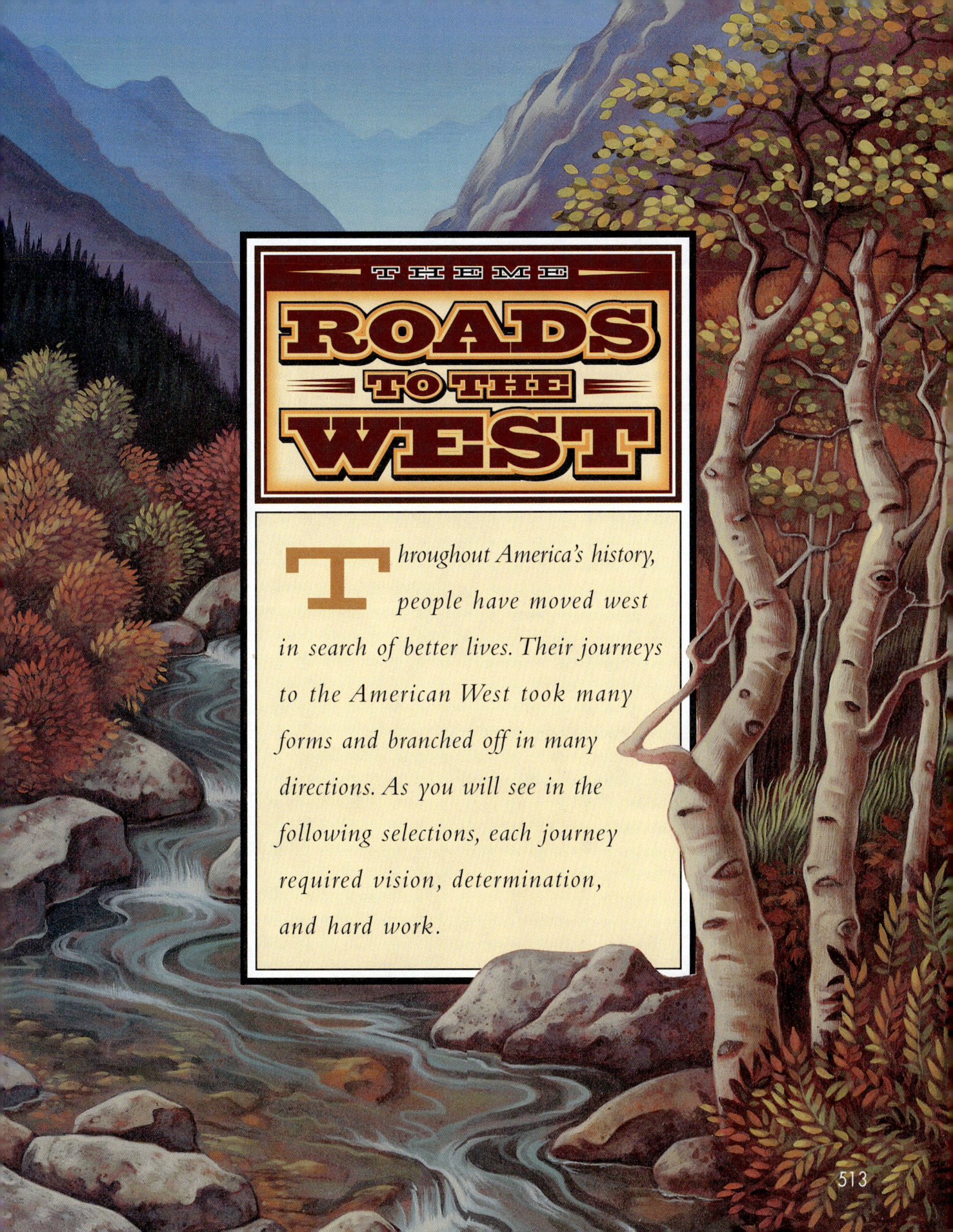

THEME
ROADS
TO THE
WEST

Throughout America's history, people have moved west in search of better lives. Their journeys to the American West took many forms and branched off in many directions. As you will see in the following selections, each journey required vision, determination, and hard work.

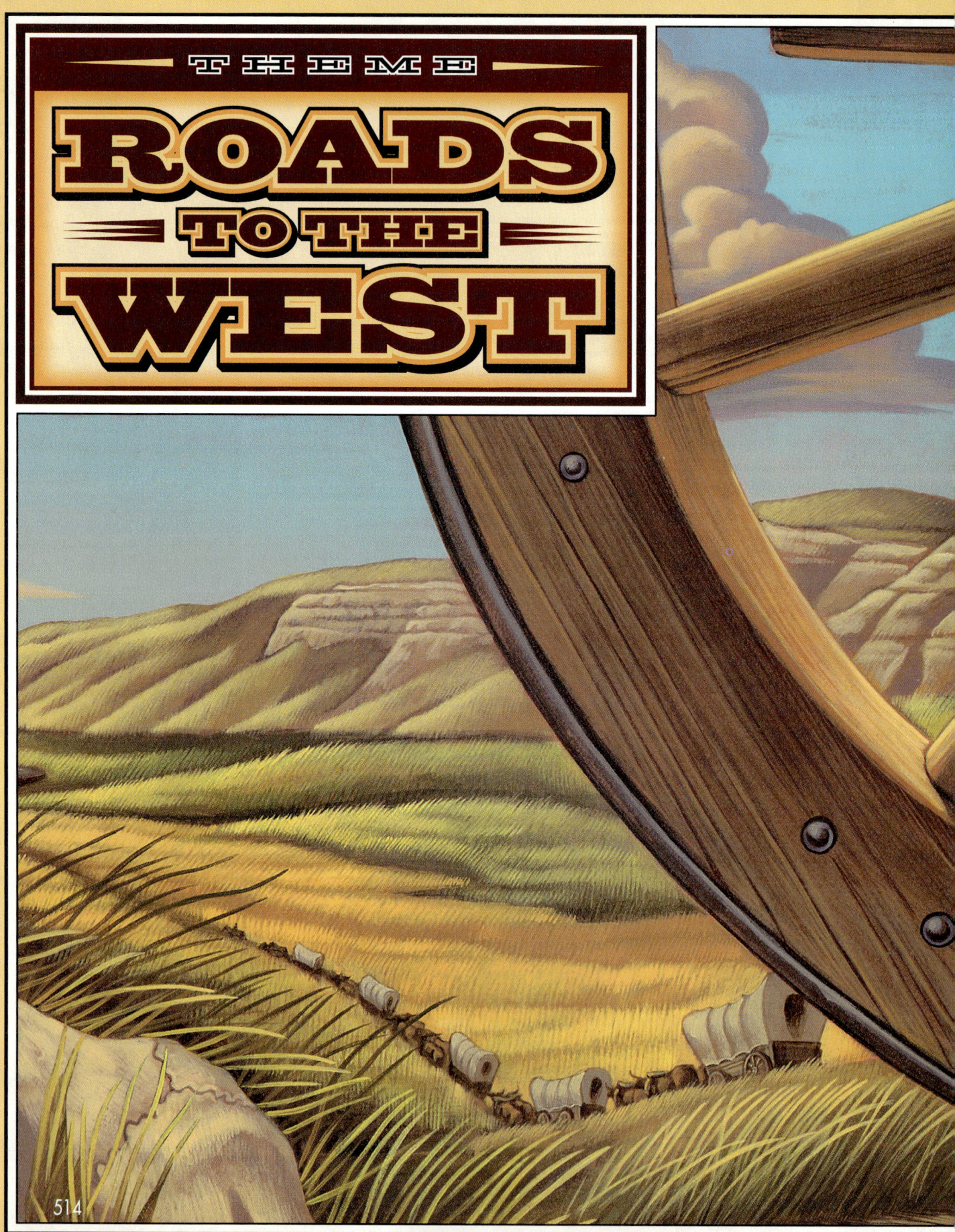

THEME

ROADS TO THE WEST

CONTENTS

BOOKSHELF

Sarah, Plain and Tall
by Patricia MacLachlan

Can a family on a prairie farm and a woman from the seacoast of Maine build a new life together?
Signatures Library

The Green Book
by Jill Paton Walsh

A spacecraft leaves the dying planet Earth to start a new civilization under the light of a new sun.
Signatures Library

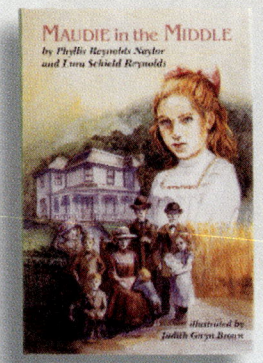

Maudie in the Middle

by Phyllis Reynolds Naylor and Laura Shield Reynolds

Young Maudie, stuck in the middle of seven siblings, feels unimportant to her family until a crisis shows her otherwise.

. . . If You Traveled West In a Covered Wagon

by Ellen Levine

How did pioneer families travel west to Oregon in covered wagons? The pioneers' tricks of survival are explained in this beautifully illustrated book.

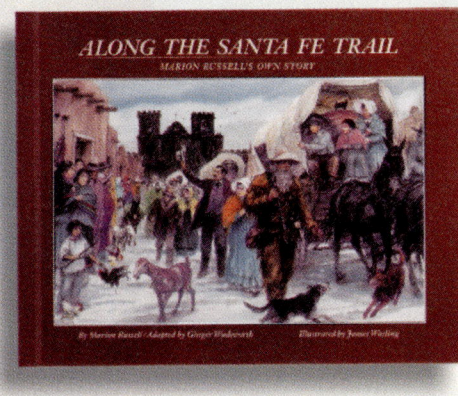

Along the Santa Fe Trail

by Marion Russell, adapted by Ginger Wadsworth

This is a true adventure story, adapted from Marion Russell's memoirs, about a family joining a wagon train bound for California.

Spanish Pioneers
of the Southwest

by Joan Anderson
photographs by George Ancona

TWENTY YEARS before the Pilgrims arrived on the east coast of North America, Don Juan de Onates led troops and settlers into the northern portion of New Spain (which is now New Mexico) to establish not only the first Spanish colony in North America but, more importantly, the first colony of Europeans in the New World. They crossed the Atlantic, landed on the east coast of Mexico (part of New Spain), and eventually traveled northward, where they were granted large parcels of land in exchange for setting up a Spanish community. In 1610, Don Pedro de Peralta founded Santa Fe and made it the capital of the new lands belonging to Spain. By the 1650s, many Spanish settlements were being established in the Southwest. The king of Spain dictated how the settlements should look and insisted that settlers build *torreones*, or round, high forts, in all of them.

This book is about one such place—El Rancho de las Golondrinas. It was owned in the 1650s by Manuel Vega y Coca and eventually fell into the hands of the Baca family. We will experience life as it was in the mid 1700s when Golondrinas was inhabited by fifty or so Baca family members. Aside from being a self-sufficient fort where the Bacas farmed and raised sheep, Golondrinas was also a hotel, or hacienda, for traders, military expeditions, and other travelers along the dangerous Camino Real.

These first colonists clung firmly to their Hispanic culture and language. Their spirit has left an indelible mark on the attitudes, values, religion, and customs of the Southwest.

The only reward in collecting wood today, Miguel thought, was that soon there would be a fiesta celebrating the coming of spring. Mamá and the other women of Golondrinas needed all the firewood that could be gathered to light the *hornos* and kitchen fireplaces. Miguel's stomach growled at the thought of food—the *dulces*, the green corn, and especially his favorite dish. He had left the hacienda at dawn with only a loaf of bread and some water. The sun was already making its westward descent toward the Sandía Mountains, which was Miguel's sign to head home.

"Come on, Gaspar," he said, nudging his faithful burro. "We've been out here long enough." Miguel tugged at his burro's reins and led Gaspar down the hillside into the valley. They trudged across the great dusty plains that served as the hacienda's backyard.

Miguel walked carefully and deliberately. He didn't want to tangle with any rattlesnakes coiled inconspicuously around desert brush, or Navajo scouts who spied on the Spanish settlers from nearby mesas.

Just last year, Miguel's brother Pedro had been taken captive in a Navajo raid. Miguel lived in fear of meeting the same fate. He shuddered every time he recalled that awful day.

All the villagers had scrambled to safety at the sound of the bell. Pedro too had run, but his pace was slowed because he carried with him a baby lamb. Miguel had watched helplessly as a Navajo scooped up his brother and rode away.

"Hurry up, Gaspar," he ordered, now more anxious than ever to get home.

It was difficult to see the hacienda from a distance, because the brown adobe fortress blended right into the landscape. Squinting hard, he finally spotted it and quickened his step, pushing Gaspar's hind end up the very last hill.

"Finally!" Miguel sighed as they approached the pine gate. "I return, Mamá," he bellowed triumphantly.

"Such a big load, Miguel!" his mother exclaimed. "And you've even cut the wood this time. *Bueno. Bueno.* Here, let me help you."

Miguel smiled at his mother's welcome. There was such relief in her eyes at his safe return. Miguel was the only Baca child old enough to help around the hacienda. His little sister, Rosa, spent her days at play, and baby Juan was just six weeks old.

Everywhere in the *placita* the people of Golondrinas were busy working. Because Nuevo Mexico was so far away from any city, they had to make everything they needed for daily life.

Doña María, the *patrón*'s wife, was brightening up a simple muslin *colcha* with embroidery, while her husband, Don Hernando, was working over the wooden loom, weaving fabric from which heavy blankets and ponchos would be fashioned. Margarita, the *patrón*'s sister, was carding freshly sheared lamb's wool, and Tía Lupita, Miguel's aunt, was hanging goat's-milk cheese from the beams in the cool storage room, where fruits and vegetables were being dried.

Just as Miguel was about to settle into a warm corner and rest his weary limbs, his father approached.

"Miguel, you've returned," he exclaimed. "I've been scanning the land all afternoon in hopes of spotting you," he said, gesturing at the wilderness beyond the gate. "You must not have met up with any grizzlies this time?" Emilio Baca joked.

"No, Papá, I didn't go up on the mesa. But if I had, I would have been ready with my knife."

"If you weren't near the mesa, wherever did you find so many juniper and piñon branches?"

"The hills west of here, Papá."

"West!" his father said. "That's getting close to Navajo country!"

"I know, Papá, but I stay alert and so far I haven't seen one Indian."

"You're becoming very brave, Miguel," his father continued, shaking his head in amazement at his young son. "The *patrón* says that he wants to give you duty in the *torreón*."

"Me?" Miguel gasped. "Stand watch like a soldier? Do you think I'm able?" he asked, straightening his spine and feeling a new rush of energy.

"Anyone who braves mesa tops and can fend off grizzly bears is man enough to guard our home. Come, enough talk," Emilio Baca said, putting his arm around his son's shoulder. "It's time for our meal. I will remind the *patrón* of his suggestion, but not until you have helped in plowing the field. The past few years your brother Pedro helped me. Now that he is gone I must look to you, Miguel."

It was warm and cozy in the Bacas' *cocina*. The chili stew smelled delectable as the family gathered and Abuelita Luisa dished it up. Everyone sat quietly, exhausted but content to be slowing down from the toils of the day.

The chill of the night descended upon them. Emilio Baca built up the fire as his wife, Isabel, unrolled the blankets and sheepskins that would become their beds. Miguel's father took his place atop the fireplace, and the others huddled close to the hearth.

Miguel felt his muscles relax as his mother began to sing softly to the baby. For the first time all day, Miguel knew he was safe. Only here in the cozy *cocina* did he feel he could let his guard down. He couldn't let Papá know that he wasn't all that brave. So on the outside, Miguel stood tall and proud, but on the inside he trembled with fear.

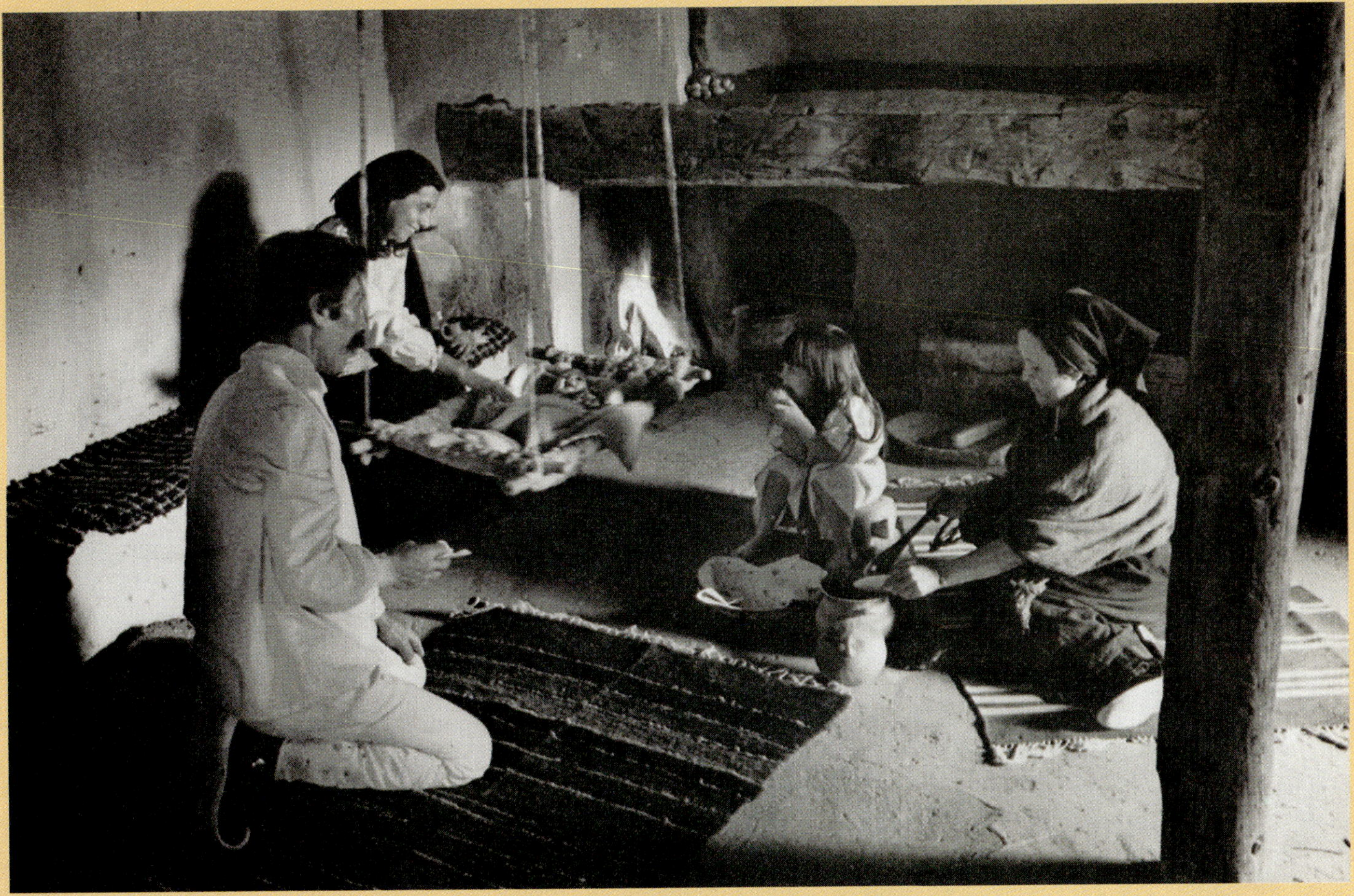

Dawn came early. With only a few tiny windows in the Bacas' *cocina*, it was impossible to know when the sun came up. But the *patrón* took care that the people of Golondrinas were alerted to the early hour by ringing the hacienda's huge iron bell.

Miguel stirred upon hearing the dull clang. One. Two. Three. Four. Five. On the fifth ring he bolted upright. Glancing about the room he saw that Papá's bed was vacant! Was he already at work? Miguel quickly rolled up his blanket, gulped down a cup of *atole,* and headed out the door.

Sure enough, Papá was down by the stream near the small plot of cultivated farmland. Miguel ran as fast as he could, anxious to show his father that even though he wasn't as big and strong as Pedro, he was eager to work.

"I'm here, Papá," he announced. "What shall I do?"

"Quickly, grab hold of the yoke while I secure it to their horns. These beasts want nothing of work this morning."

Miguel did as his father said, and eventually they attached the crude wooden plow and headed for the far end of the field. The earth was hard and dry. Miguel was always amazed that things grew in such unhealthy-looking soil.

"Papá," he asked, his teeth chattering in the early morning chill, "isn't it still too cold for planting?"

"It would seem so, my son," Emilio Baca answered as the plowshare dug into

524

the soil and began to turn the earth. "But we must hope that the days soon become warm, as it takes many months to grow our corn and beans and wheat. Besides, Padre José will come to bless our fields during the Feast of San Ysidro. If we haven't done our work there can be no blessing, *sí*?"

"I suppose not, Papá," Miguel answered, working steadily now. It felt good to be sharing chores with someone instead of being alone tending sheep and collecting wood. Time passed quickly, and by late afternoon they were putting in the seed. Miguel felt proud of their accomplishment, especially since the

"We must open up the irrigation ditch, *sí*, Miguel? Your newly planted seeds will be crying for moist soil."

"*Sí, señor*," Miguel answered, grabbing a long stick and pushing with all his might the board that held the water back. Suddenly it gave way and the sparkling-clean water gushed forth, heading straight for the field.

"We must make good use of this water, my boy, since we have so very little, *sí*?" The *patrón* slapped Miguel on the back, pleased that another job was done.

"Come, let's head back to the hacienda," the *patrón* said to his young helper.

patrón had been watching their progress from the rooftop of the hacienda.

Just as Miguel was placing the last of the seeds in the carefully dug holes, a voice called to him. "Miguel, come give me a hand."

Miguel dropped the seed bag and ran. Whenever the *patrón* had a request, the villagers obliged. He was, after all, the owner of Golondrinas—the person to whom they all turned for food and favors. It was an honor to help him in return.

"Look how full our stream is, after the winter's snow," he said, his voice booming, as it always did, with great joy.

During the next few days, Miguel went about his regular chores hoping that soon the *patrón* would remember his promise and permit him to stand watch in the *torreón*.

Each morning he tossed fresh straw into the corral for the barn animals to eat. He fed the chickens and turkeys, milked the goats, and held the sheep steady while they were sheared.

In the afternoons, sometimes with his father, sometimes alone, he took the sheep to the nearby hills to graze. The days were long and hard, and Miguel began to wonder why there seemed to be more work this spring than in other years. Then he realized—Pedro wasn't there this year to share in all the work.

One afternoon, while he mixed the reddish-brown earth with straw and water to make adobe bricks, Miguel heard the thunder of hooves as a horse galloped toward the hacienda. Jumping to attention, he shielded his eyes from the dust and watched as a Pueblo Indian passed by.

The Pueblos were a friendly people whom the Spanish settlers had learned

to cooperate with. They brought pottery, baskets, and fruit to the hacienda to exchange for sheepskins and sugar. Miguel marveled at how the Pueblo men wore little clothing and seemed unaffected by the cold weather. He crept up to the pine gate and nestled unobtrusively in the corner, hoping to eavesdrop on Margarita's conversation. Miguel

took any chance he could to understand the mysterious world of the Indians, especially now that his brother was part of that world.

"Have you visited any Navajo villages of late?" Margarita whispered to the Pueblo. Miguel moved closer as the Pueblo nodded yes. "By chance did you spot our beloved Pedro?" she pressed.

529

"No, no, no," he answered, a sad tone to his voice.

"Well then," she said, trying to cover up her disappointment, "let us see what you have brought today."

Miguel watched as the Indian showed Margarita brightly colored baskets and sturdy pottery jugs, but his interest in Indian things had been suddenly dampened.

"If only I were big enough to go off and find Pedro," Miguel said, sighing. "Perhaps when I learn to handle the muskets in the *torreón* I will be able to rescue him."

The very next morning the *patrón*, Don Hernando, stopped by the Baca *cocina* and assigned Miguel to the morning watch.

His head brimming with thoughts of fighting off Indians, and his heart pounding at the thought of a dramatic rescue of his brother, Miguel climbed the rickety ladder leading to the tower. Feeling like his conquistador ancestors, he stepped out into the open and gazed

over the rugged landscape. He felt nervous about the responsibility given to him. Pacing about behind the small parapet, he rehearsed in his mind just what he was supposed to do in case of attack.

The strains of the *alabados* being sung by the women in the chapel beneath him caused Miguel to relax a bit, knowing that prayers were being offered for protection from the forces of evil.

In the distance he could see the Indian servant, Polonia, with her little girl trailing behind, fetching water from the stream. For the first time Miguel wondered what had possessed the *patrón* to take Polonia captive, and why she now seemed so content with the Spanish way of life. Didn't she miss the Indian ways? Could Pedro be experiencing the same thing? Might he be taking to the Navajo way of life? There was so much Miguel didn't understand.

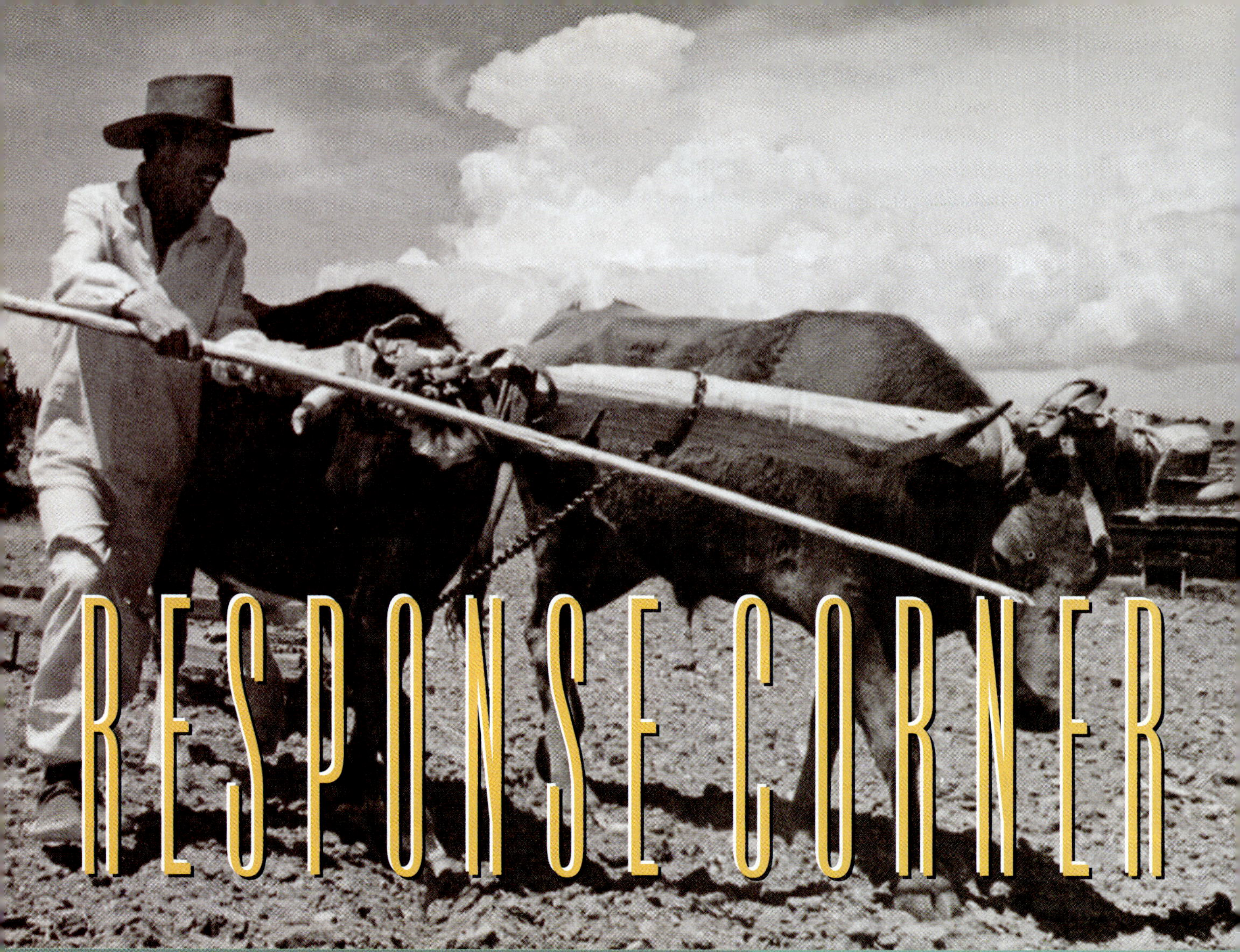

RESPONSE CORNER

CREATE FLASHCARDS

SPANISH IN A FLASH

Work with a partner to make a deck of flashcards with the Spanish words from the selection on one side and their English meanings on the other side. Shuffle the deck and quiz each other. Continue until each of you knows all the Spanish words.

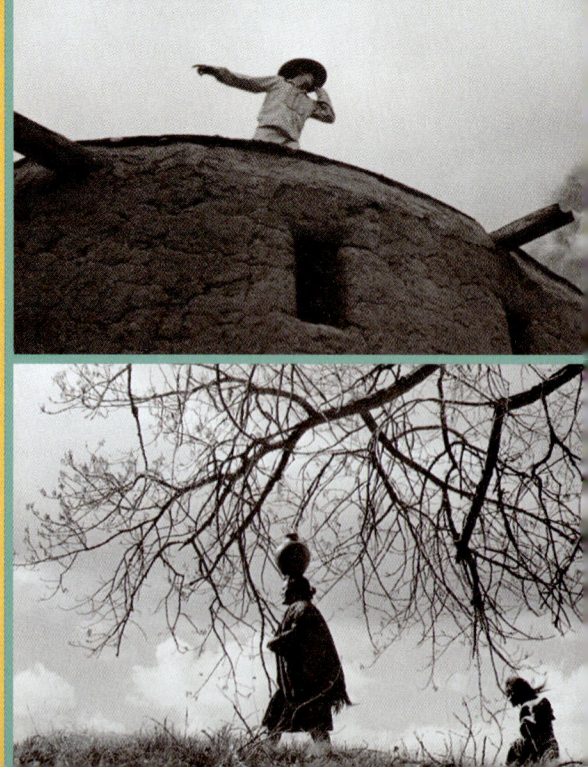

NECESSITIES OF LIFE

Pioneers such as Miguel and his family had to produce everything they needed to live. Work with a partner. List the items from the modern world that you would miss the most if you had to be completely self-sufficient.

TIME TRAVELER

Imagine that you are able to travel back in time to Miguel's village. Write an action adventure story about what happens. Share your story with your classmates.

WHAT DO YOU THINK?

· How do you know that Miguel and his family are brave pioneers?

· Has this selection changed your opinion about pioneer life?

· In what ways is Miguel's life similar to yours? In what ways is it different?

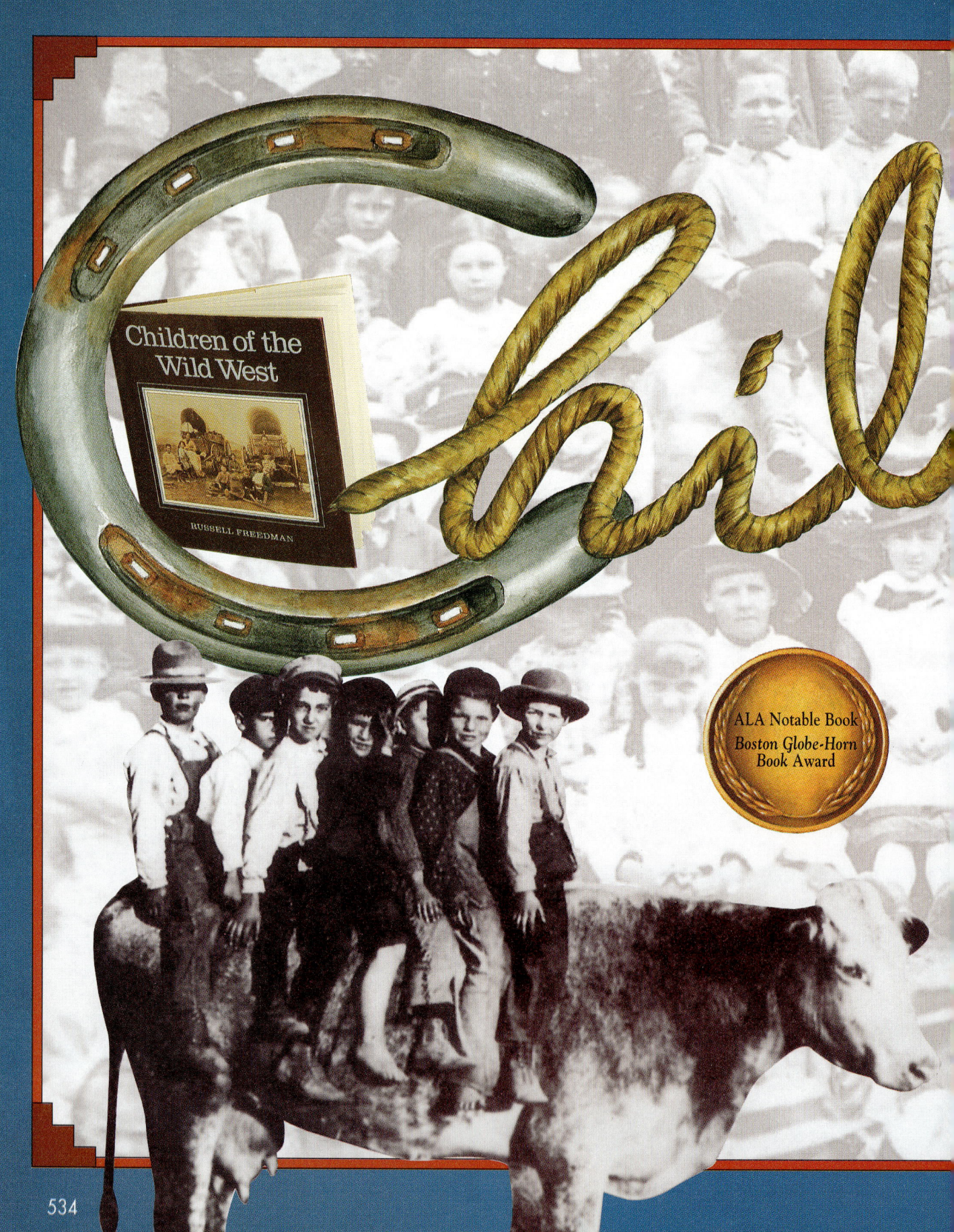

Children of the
Wild West

RUSSELL FREEDMAN

ALA Notable Book
*Boston Globe-Horn
Book Award*

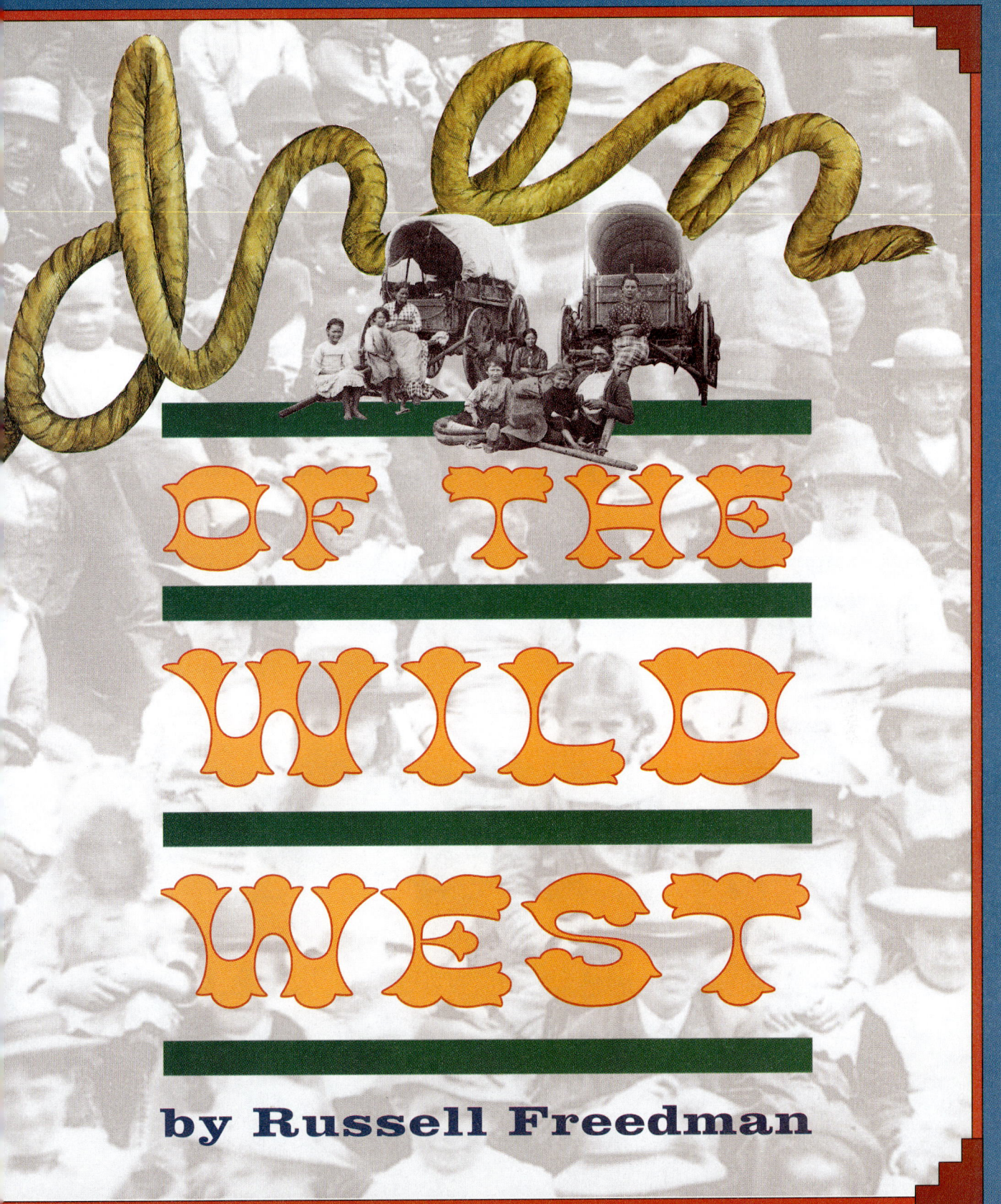

Children

OF THE

WILD

WEST

by Russell Freedman

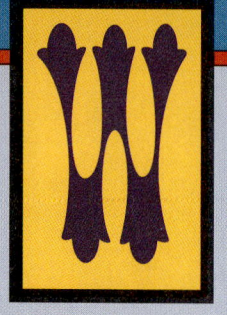

When settlers first moved into an area, there were no schools of any kind. Children were taught at home, or at the home of a neighbor. A pioneer woman would take time from her endless tasks to gather a circle of children around her and teach them reading, writing, and arithmetic. Lacking a blackboard, she used a long stick to scratch out letters and numbers on the dirt floor of the family cabin.

As soon as there were enough children in an area, families would band together to put up a proper school.

Everyone contributed labor and materials for the schoolhouse, which often served as a church on Sundays.

The first schoolhouse was usually a simple cabin built of logs, sod, or adobe. Each morning students were called to class by the iron bell that hung outside the schoolhouse door. They came by foot, on horseback, and in wagons, carrying their books, their slates and tablets, and their dinner pails. Some of them had to travel several miles in each direction.

Youngsters of all ages were taught by a single teacher.

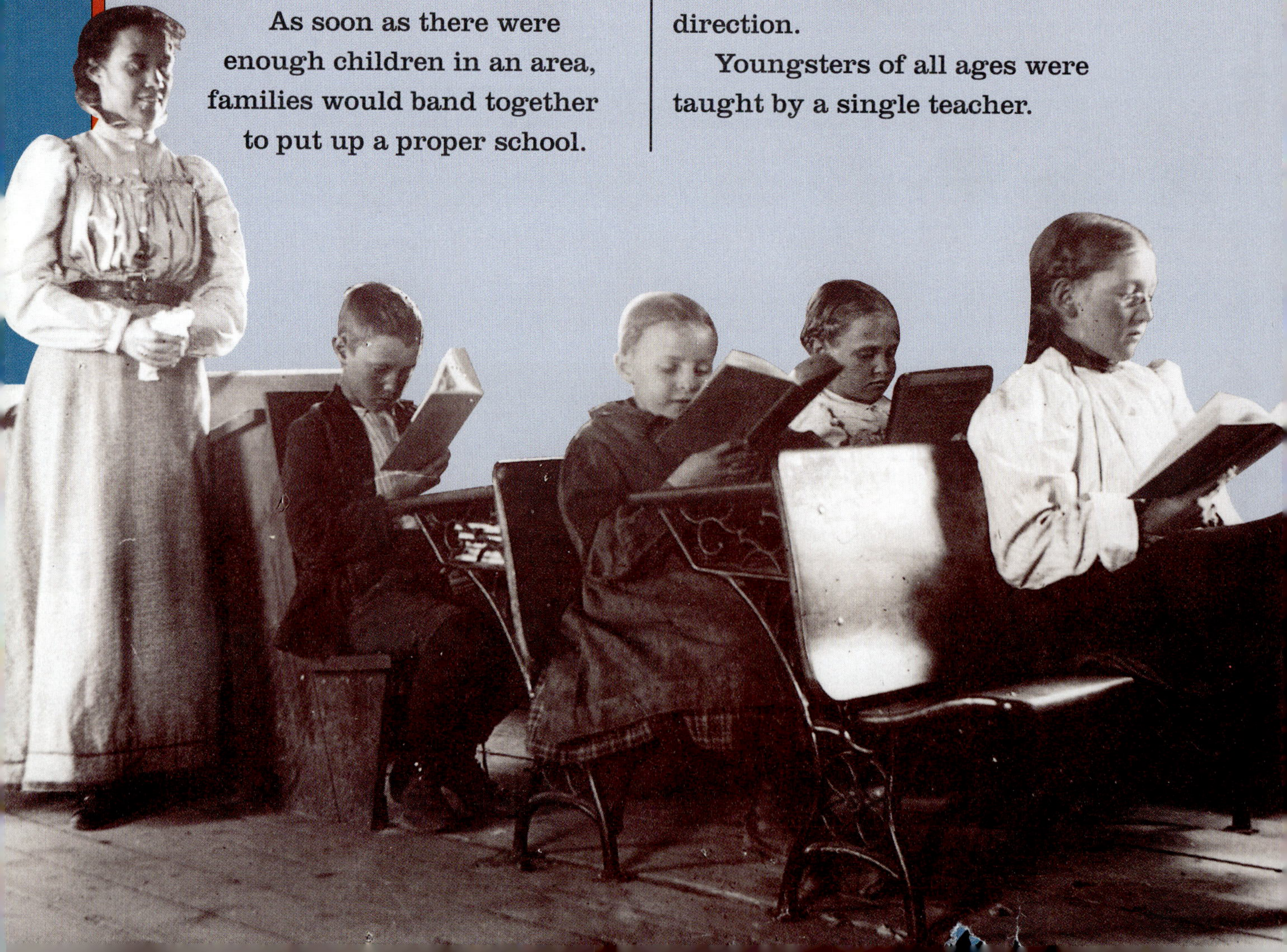

Schools, like frontier homes, sometimes had dirt floors. Since there was no running water, everyone drank from the same bucket and dipper kept in a corner of the room. The "playground" was the field outside. The "rest room" was an outhouse. Dogs of many breeds and sizes hung around the schoolhouse, whining at the door and sneaking inside to lie at their owners' feet.

Some early schools had no blackboards, no charts, maps or globes, no special equipment of any kind. Since textbooks were scarce, students brought whatever books they had at home. They arrived at school with an assortment of dictionaries, histories, encyclopedias, and storybooks. Many had copies of McGuffey's Readers, popular schoolbooks of the day that were filled with inspiring stories about hard work, honesty, and piety. Other students might have only a family Bible or an old almanac for their reading lessons.

Much of the classroom time was devoted to the three Rs, along with American history and geography. Students memorized grammar rules, recited history dates, practiced penmanship and arithmetic tables, read aloud, and competed in spelling bees. Since

ABOVE: A SOD SCHOOLHOUSE
LEFT: THE READING LESSON

the pupils might range in age from seven or eight to sixteen or older, they were not separated into grades. The teacher worked with one or two students at a time, while the others studied by themselves. Older students often tutored younger ones.

The youngsters attended classes only as their chores and the weather allowed. On an ordinary school day, many youngsters were up at 4 A.M., milking cows, chopping wood, toting water, and helping fix breakfast before leaving for school. After a full day of classes, they might do other chores by moonlight so as not to miss the next day's classes.

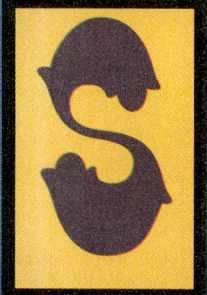ince some children lived miles away from the nearest school, they might not attend classes at all until they were half grown. It was not uncommon to find youngsters twelve or fourteen years old who were just starting school for the first time. During the 1860s, fewer than half the youngsters in Oregon received any formal schooling. California did not make education compulsory until 1874, when a law was passed requiring children between the ages of eight and fourteen to attend classes during at least two-thirds of the school year.

Many frontier schools found it difficult to find and keep good teachers. The pay was low. A teacher might earn anywhere from

GETTING READY TO BOARD THE SCHOOL BUS

ten dollars to thirty-five dollars a month, paid only while school was in session. In some areas, the school year lasted only three or four months.

To help make up for the low pay, teachers often received free room and board. They lived with the families of their pupils, moving from one home to another, staying longest with families that had the most children in school. Since so many pioneer families lived in small crowded cabins, this system could be tough on the teacher.

Few teachers had any formal training. To receive a teaching certificate, they had only to pass simple examinations in basic subjects. Some schools were glad to accept almost anyone who was willing to take on the job.

Teachers were especially hard to find in California's mining camps. At a mining town in Tuolumne County, an unsuccessful gold-seeker named Prentice Mulford applied for a teaching job. He was examined by the school trustees—a doctor, a miner, and a saloonkeeper. "I expected a searching examination, and trembled," Mulford recalled. "It was years since I had seen a schoolbook. I knew that in geography I was rusty and in mathematics musty. Before the doctor lay one thin book. It turned out to be a spelling book."

Mulford was asked to spell *cat, hat, rat,* and *mat.* When he did this perfectly, the doctor told him, "Young man, you're hired."

Not all frontier schoolteachers could spell as perfectly as young Mulford. In 1859, the superintendent of schools in Sacramento, California, complained that some teachers were misspelling the name of the state they were teaching in as *Callifornia* or *Calafornia.*

Some teachers were barely older than their pupils. Often they hoped to learn as much as they taught. In 1855, Charles A. Murdock organized the first public school in Arcata, California:

RIGHT: SCHOOL DISTRICT NO. 32

BELOW: THIS WELL-EQUIPPED CLASSROOM HAD A BIG CAST-IRON STOVE AND A REAL BLACKBOARD.

"There was no school in the town when we came. It troubled my mother that my brother and sister must be without lessons. Several other small children also were deprived of the opportunity. In the emergency we cleaned out a room in the store . . . and I organized a very primary school.

"I was almost fifteen, but the children were good and manageable. I did not have very many, and fortunately I was not called upon to teach very long. There came to town a clever man, Robert Desty. He wanted to teach. There was no school building, but he built one all by his own hands. He suggested that I give up my school and become a pupil of his. I was very glad to do it. He was a good and ingenious teacher. I enjoyed his lessons about six months, and then I felt I must help my father."

Eventually school boards began to adopt rules that no teacher under sixteen years of age could be hired. As late as 1880, however, the United States Census reported that California still had one boy and two girl teachers under sixteen.

LUNCHTIME: AN OLD TOBACCO TIN AND A LARD PAIL SERVE AS THE GIRLS' LUNCH BOXES.

Russell Freedman

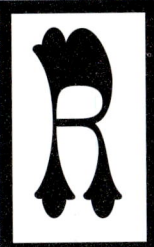 ussell Freedman grew up in San Francisco, California, surrounded by books. Because his father worked in publishing, famous authors would often visit his home. He recalls, "I knew at an early age that I wanted to be a writer, like those strange, wonderful men and women who sat at our dinner table telling stories that were always fascinating, and sometimes hard to believe."

When Freedman was older, he worked for a time as a newspaper reporter. There he learned skills that helped him become one of America's best writers of nonfiction for young people.

Freedman tries to make his readers care about a subject by telling about it as simply and clearly as possible. He also tries to spark the reader's imagination by telling a good story. He says, "Pick a subject, a good subject, and you're sure to find kids who are interested in it."

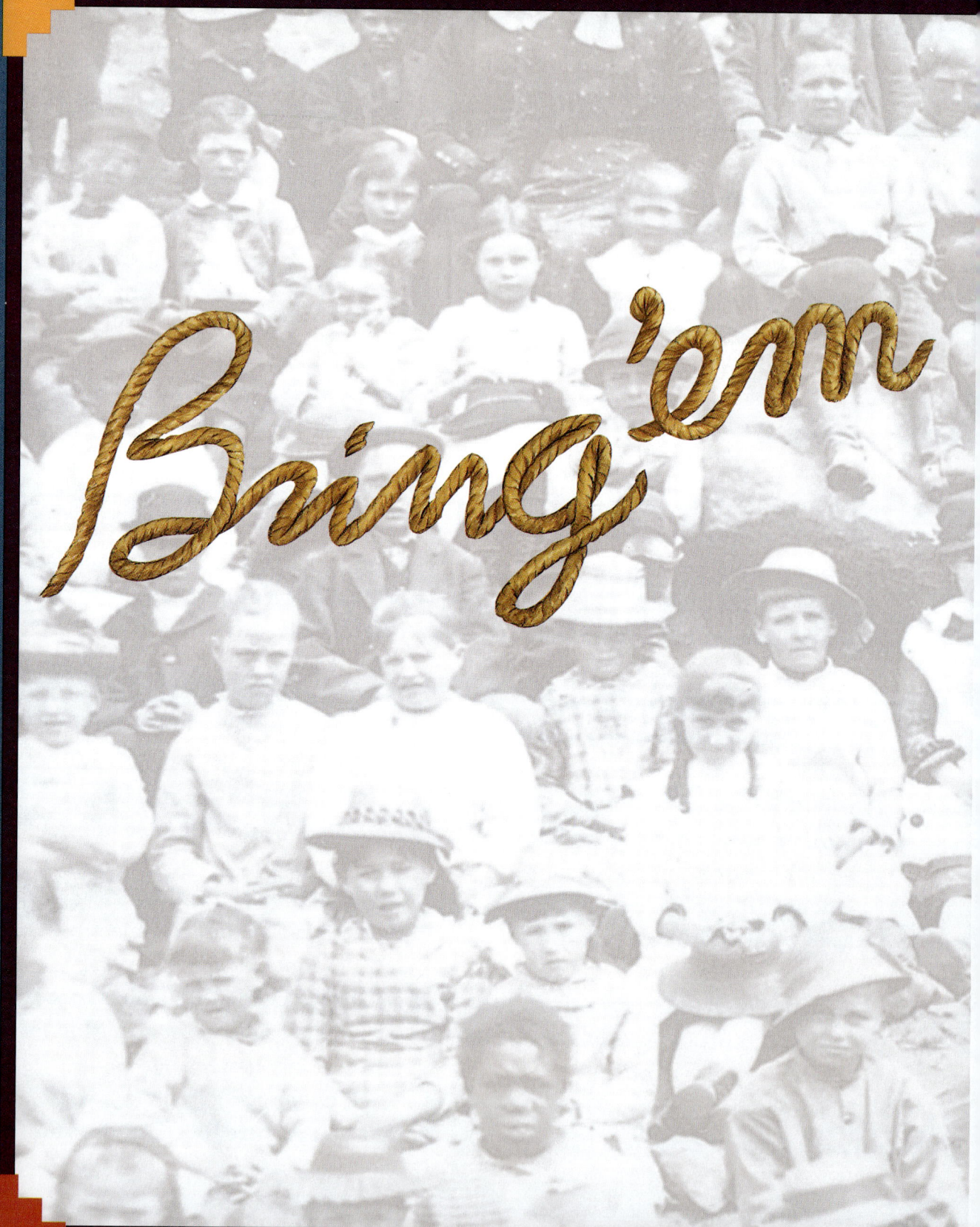

Bring 'em

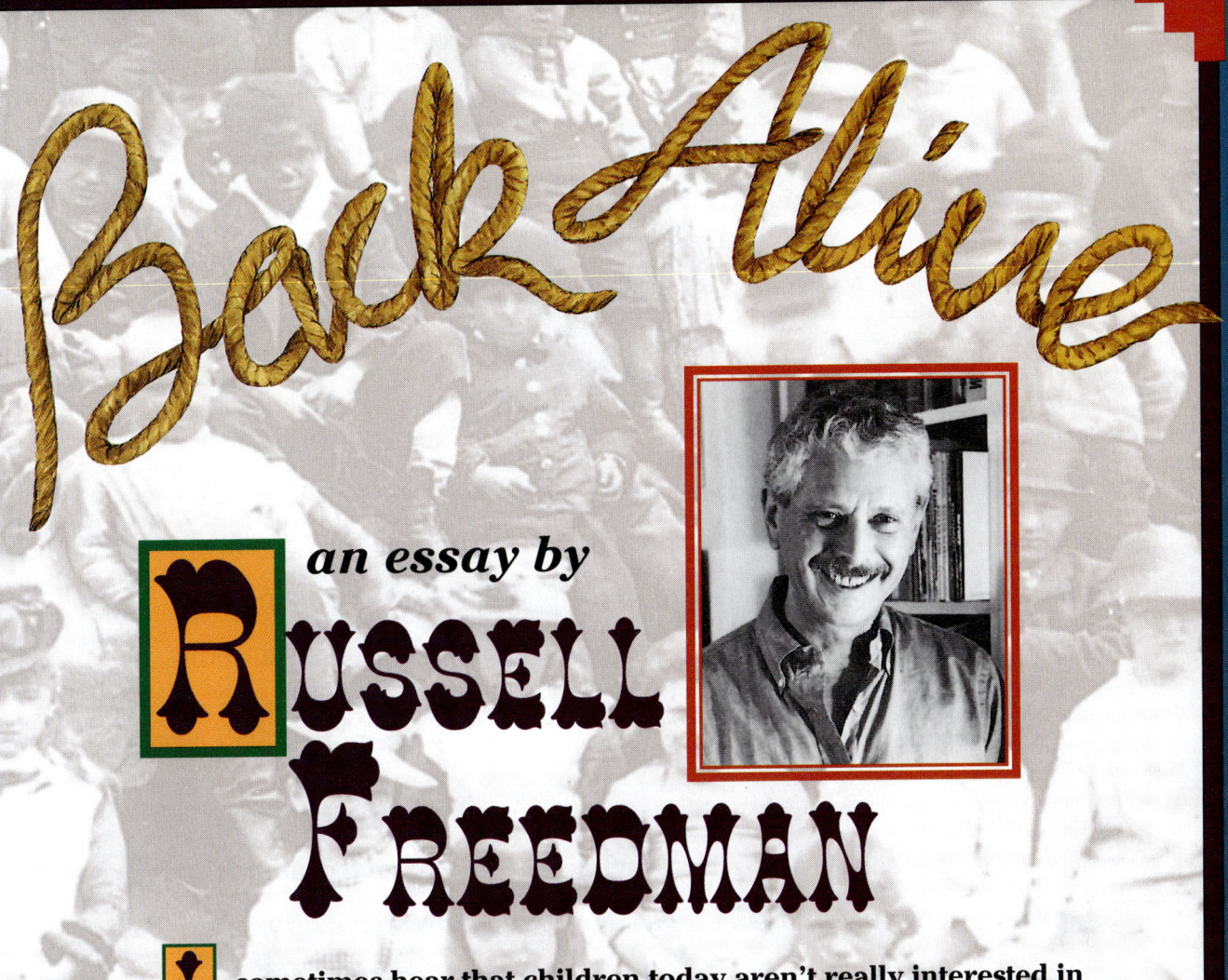

Back Alive

an essay by RUSSELL FREEDMAN

I sometimes hear that children today aren't really interested in history. It's one of their least favorite subjects. They look upon history as a kind of castor oil that one has to take—something that's good for you, maybe, but repulsive.

If that attitude exists, then it can only result from the way history is taught. I believe that history can be far more exciting than any imaginary adventure story because truth is so much stranger than fiction. Rather than castor oil, history should be thought of as a tonic. It should wake us up, because it is the story of ourselves.

The word *history*, remember, is made up mostly of the word *story*. Historians traditionally have been storytellers. Going all the way back to Homer and beyond, historians have been people who were telling, singing, reciting epic poems. They were storytellers sitting around the fire inside the cave, holding their audience spellbound on a winter's night.

When I begin a new book, I like to remember that tradition. I think of myself first of all as a storyteller, and I do my best to give dramatic shape to my subject, whatever it is. I always feel that I have a story to tell that is worth telling, and I want to tell it as clearly, as simply, and as forcefully as I can.

Nonfiction can and does make use of traditional story-telling techniques. One of the most effective techniques, for example, is to create a vivid, detailed scene that the reader can visualize—like a scene from a movie, if you will. In my book *Children of the Wild West* (Clarion, 1983), I use that device to help establish the setting and the mood, and to pull the reader into the story. After a short introduction, the book's opening chapter begins like this:

It was a typical wagon train of the 1840s. The swaying wagons, plodding animals, and walking people stretched out along the trail for almost a mile.

Near the end of the train, a boy holding a hickory stick moved slowly through the dust. He used the stick to poke and prod the cows that trudged beside him, mooing and complaining. "Get along!" he shouted. "Hey! Hey! Get along!"

Dust floated in the air. It clogged the boy's nose, parched his throat, and coated his face. His cheeks were smeared where he had brushed away the big mosquitoes that buzzed about everywhere.

Up ahead, his family's wagon bounced down the trail. He would hear the "crack" of his father's whip above the heads of the oxen that pulled the wagon. The animals coughed and snorted. The chains on their yokes rattled with every step they took.

Now, that is nonfiction. The scene is dramatized in order to make it visual, and in order to convey the texture and flavor of the event and the time. But it is entirely factual. And it introduces the story line —the narrative framework—of the book. *Children of the Wild West* is the story of children who accompanied their parents on the great westward journey, and the story of what happened to them after they arrived in the West.

Backwoods Scholars

from *A Pioneer Sampler*
by Barbara Greenwood

illustrated by Mercedes McDonald

Letters and numbers—that's what most pioneer children learned. They scratched the alphabet onto slates with slate pencils as they learned to write. Later they graduated to homemade ink, quill pens, and paper brought from home.

They learned arithmetic that would help them with everyday life. Adding and subtracting were used to determine their accounts at the general store. Multiplying and dividing helped them figure the size of a field or the number of cords in a pile of wood.

Children attended school until they were twelve or until they had learned the "rule of three," a method for finding the size of an object too large to measure easily. Early settlers needed to know how to use this rule to find heights of trees and distances across rivers.

This is how the rule of three works: Willy Robertson's father was going to cut down a tree near the cabin. To make sure it would not fall on the house and buildings, he needed to know how tall it was.

First he drove a stick into the ground. He measured the length of the stick from the ground up and the length of the stick's shadow. Next he measured the length of the tree's shadow. Now he had the three numbers he needed to find the unknown fourth.

The stick was one length long.

Its shadow was two lengths long.

The tree's shadow was thirty lengths long.

To find the height of the tree, he wrote:

	$\dfrac{\text{stick length}}{\substack{\text{stick}\\ \text{shadow length}}}$		$\dfrac{\text{tree height}}{\substack{\text{tree}\\ \text{shadow length}}}$
or	$\frac{1}{2}$	=	$\frac{x}{30}$
or	$2x$	=	30
or	x	=	15 lengths

So, using the rule of three, Mr. Robertson learned that the tree was fifteen lengths tall. Now he could measure this distance along the ground to see if the tree would fall too close to the cabin.

RESPONSE
Corner

SCHOOL SETTINGS

Make a comparison chart. On one side, list the good and bad points of going to school. On the other side, do the same for being taught at home. Which form of schooling do you think is better and why? Share your thoughts with your classmates.

DEBATE AN ISSUE

LAW AND ORDER

In 1874, the state of California said that all children ages 8 to 14 had to go to school for two-thirds of the school year. Put yourself in the place of a student in 1874. Hold a debate with classmates about the fairness of the law.

550

YOU WERE THERE

Russell Freedman believes that history can be shared in the form of interesting adventure stories. Research and share a true story from the Wild West. Tell the story using the words and actions of a child who lived back then.

WHAT DO YOU THINK?

- What did you learn about frontier schools that you had never thought about before?

- What surprised you about teachers in frontier schools?

- How might the essay "Bring 'em Back Alive" contribute to your enjoyment of "Children of the Wild West"?

You have read about people who began new lives by moving west. What does the painting *Among the Sierra Nevada Mountains, California* tell you about the excitement these people might have felt about their new lives? What does it show you about the hardships they may have faced while crossing a continent?

Among the Sierra Nevada Mountains, California
by Albert Bierstadt

Albert Bierstadt was born in Germany in 1830, but he grew up in Massachusetts. In 1857 he joined a team sent to map a route from St. Louis, Missouri, to the Pacific Ocean. He was amazed by the spectacular scenery of the West. Two years later he began showing his landscapes of the area. His work was well liked, and his paintings were bought by many collectors. In 1875 Congress purchased one of his landscapes, and it still hangs in the Capitol.

Oil on canvas, 1868, National Museum of American Art, Washington, DC

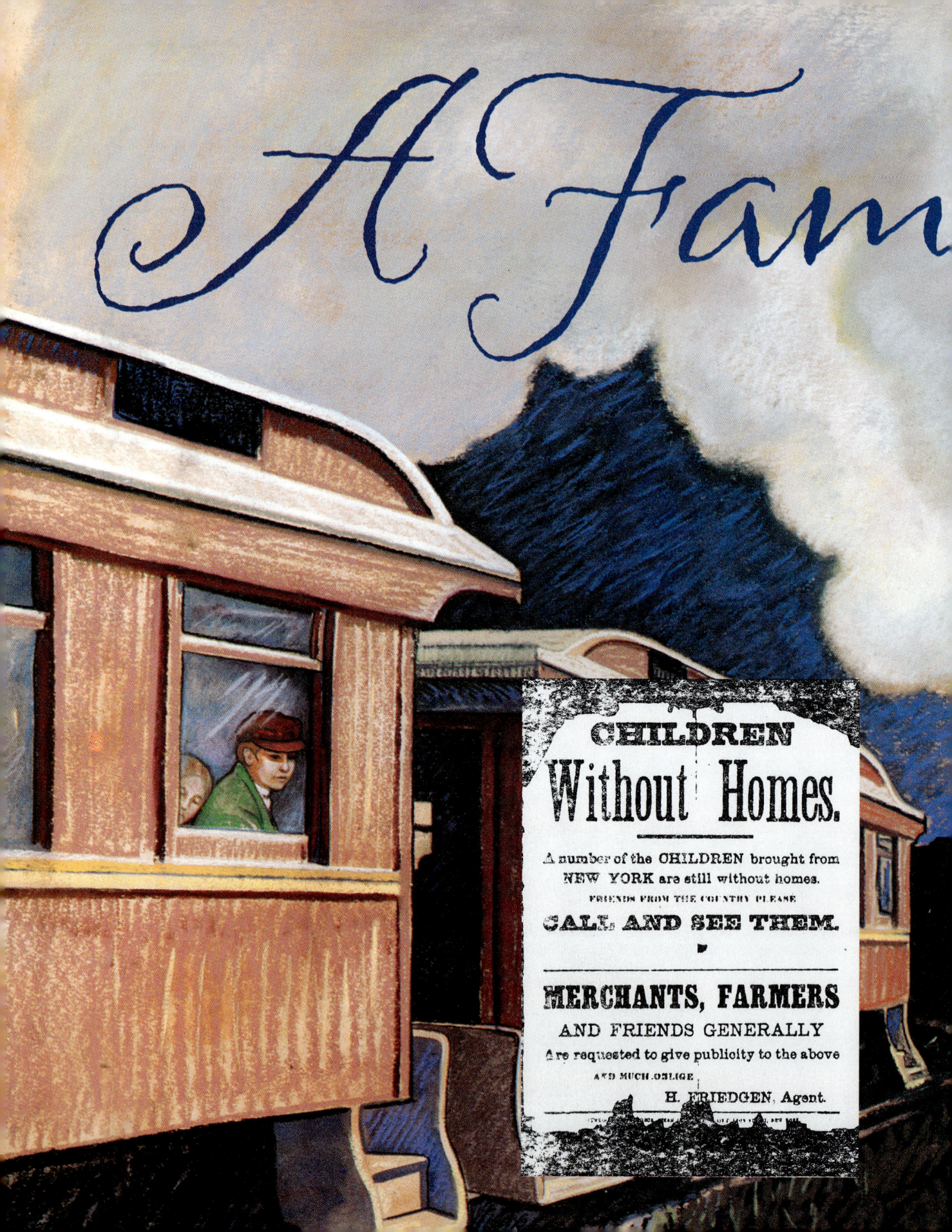

A Fam

CHILDREN
Without Homes.

A number of the CHILDREN brought from
NEW YORK are still without homes.
FRIENDS FROM THE COUNTRY PLEASE
CALL AND SEE THEM.

MERCHANTS, FARMERS
AND FRIENDS GENERALLY
Are requested to give publicity to the above
AND MUCH OBLIGE
H. FRIEDGEN, Agent.

ily Apart

The Orphan Train Quartet

By Joan Lowery Nixon • illustrated by Pamela Patrick

Award-Winning
Author

When Mr. Kelly dies, Mrs. Kelly realizes she cannot properly provide for six children, ages 6 to 13. As many people in the late 1800s did, she sends her children west to Missouri on the "orphan train" in hopes that they will be placed with families who can give them better opportunities.

Frances Kelly, the eldest child, leaves New York on a train with her three brothers and two sisters. Frances has heard that families often choose boys to do farm work, and she wants to be picked with Petey, the youngest child. So Frances has convinced the guides, Andrew and Katherine, that she is Frankie Kelly, a boy.

The train started up in its usual bumping fashion. It was late and dark, with only the dim light from the swinging lantern casting wild, moving shadows across the car. As Frances stared out at the landscape, she could see clustered lights of houses that winked through the night. Then the lights became more scattered, until finally there was nothing outside the train but a black, empty world without moonlight or stars.

Frances shifted under the weight of Petey's head on her lap and leaned against the wooden frame of the window, closing her eyes. Megan sniffled beside her, and she reached over to take her hand.

"I keep thinking about what Andrew said," Megan whispered, "about how people don't take all the children in a family. We're going to be sent to different homes. It frightens me. Does it frighten you, too?"

"Yes," Frances said, keeping her voice low. "It does."

"I don't want to think about being parted from you," Megan said. "We've always been together."

Frances squeezed Megan's hand. "Maybe we won't be parted. Maybe someone will say, 'We want all those fine Kelly children!' And they'll take us to their house— a big white house with green—no, blue—shutters, and they'll have a horse for Petey to ride and—"

Megan interrupted. "None of your dreams now, Frances. Dreams are just pretending, and you know they don't come true."

"I wish this one could." Frances groaned. "Oh, if only Ma hadn't—"

But Megan interrupted, her voice breaking. "Please don't talk about Ma now. I miss her too much."

They were silent for a few minutes, and soon Megan fell asleep, her head resting heavily on Frances's shoulder. One of the smaller children in the car was crying, and Frances could hear Katherine's low, comforting murmur. Before long the only sounds in the car were the creaks and groans of the wooden seats and the clatter of iron wheels against the rails, all of which flowed into a steady rhythm. Soon Frances was sound asleep.

"WAKE UP, FRANKIE. I want to go home."

Frances awoke stiff and tired as Petey buried his face in her neck, whimpering, "I want Ma!"

"I want Ma, too! Are we ever going to see Ma again?" Peg wailed.

"There, now," Frances soothed, "of course we are." But she kept her eyes downcast, unable to meet theirs. How could she tell them this when she didn't believe it herself? Every turn of the train's wheels took them farther and farther away from Ma. Frances tried to smile, to bolster their spirits, because she was in charge. The others mustn't know that she felt like crying, too.

Frances looked up, feeling Megan's appraising eyes upon her.

Megan brushed back her long, dark hair and whispered, "What will happen to us, Frankie?"

"Why—we'll find good homes. We'll have new families and good food and warm beds," Frances parroted. She reached across Petey and gripped her sister's hand. "Oh, Megan," she whispered, "I honestly don't know what will happen."

One of the younger boys fell into the aisle and let out a yell. At the sound of it another child began to cry.

"Can't someone shut those urchins up!" Mr. Crandon bellowed as the train lurched into motion.

"They're only children," a woman snapped at him.

Mr. Crandon puffed up like a pigeon guarding the only crumb of bread. "Madam, we are entitled to as much peace and quiet as this railroad company can provide."

"I'm sorry." Andrew raised his voice over the din. "We'll feed the children at the next stop, and I can guarantee that will help the situation."

"If you can't control them—" Mr. Crandon began.

But Mike suddenly jumped into the aisle and shouted to the older children, "Hey there, chums! How about a bit of music?" He cupped his hands together and held them against his lips, creating a lively, nasal music as he hummed, and to the music he danced a few wild steps of a jig.

The children who had been crying stopped to stare, then broke into laughter as Mike leaped to click his heels together, lost his balance, and sprawled in the aisle.

Frances saw the twinkle in Mike's eyes and knew he had taken the fall on purpose.

"More! More!" Petey shouted.

So Mike pranced and danced with his odd music, and when some of the older children recognized a tune, they joined in, singing the words. Frances knew "The Irish Washerwoman" and "Old Dog Tray," and when Mike began "Oh! Susanna," some of the adults on the car began to sing, too, Captain Taylor's deep baritone as loud as Andrew's.

Suddenly, with a jolt that tossed Mike sideways onto Katherine's lap, the train shook and rattled to a screeching stop.

"Good work," Katherine murmured to Mike as she helped him regain his balance.

Captain Taylor stretched forward to shake Mike's hand and said, "A wise choice of action, son."

Frances was proud of Mike. He'd been able to make them all forget their aches and fears. Ma would have been proud of Mike, too, if she could have seen him.

Her thoughts were interrupted by the frantic cry of "Fire!"

The conductor threw open the door of the passenger car. "Sparks from the train set a brushfire!" he shouted. "All able-bodied males are needed to help put it out!"

"Come on!" Mike grabbed Frances's arm and tugged her into the aisle. "'All able-bodied males,'" he wickedly muttered under his breath. "That means you, too!"

"Don't be frightened, boys." Andrew stopped Frances with a firm grip on her shoulder and handed her a wet feed sack as she leapt from the railroad car. "It's not uncommon for sparks to set small brushfires. Just take this sack and join the others."

Deep orange and scarlet flames crawled and crackled through the burning grass, and yellow smoke rose in choking clouds.

Most of the men and boys had poured from the train, grabbed the wet sacks, and were slapping them at the smoldering grass. Frances, hands shaking with terror, copied their actions. Working hard, slamming her dripping sack on the flames, dipping it over and over into the bucket and slamming it again, she was soon absorbed in beating back the low spurts of flame.

"Look out! You're on fire!"

Frances jumped, but it was Amos Crandon Mike meant.

Mr. Crandon froze with fear as the back of his shirttail burst into flame.

"Your shirt, man! Pull it off!" Andrew shouted and began to run toward Mr. Crandon.

But Mike was faster. He dove toward the backs of Mr. Crandon's knees. Mr. Crandon bent in two and fell over Mike, sitting down hard. Mike scrambled on top of the man and pushed him on his back, rolling him over and flinging himself across him.

Mike sat up and examined the scorched shirt. "Fire's out," he announced happily.

Mr. Crandon angrily sputtered, "How dare you push me to the ground? You ought to be whipped!"

Frances wanted to defend Mike but was too furious to do anything but sputter. She was glad that Andrew seemed as surprised as Mike by Mr. Crandon's outburst. She caught her breath as Andrew spoke up: "Your shirt was on fire. Mike put it out and kept you from getting burned."

Mr. Crandon glared at Andrew. He brushed the dirt from his clothes and, muttering to himself, unaware that two large spots of very pink skin were showing through holes in his trousers, stomped to the train.

Andrew patted Mike's shoulder, and Frances said, "You did the right thing, Mike." But it wasn't at Mike that she was looking. Andrew was a fine man, a really good and kind man like Da. Oh, how Frances yearned to be called Frances Mary again!

"On board, everybody," the conductor yelled as he collected the dirty, charred feed sacks. "Fire's out. Get back on board so we can get under way."

"After this train ride is over," Mike muttered to Frances as they climbed the steps to their car, "I hope I'll never see ol' Crandon again!"

The train rattled its way west, stopping every twenty-five miles or so for water and wood. Frances gazed dreamily out over the open hills, the dim forests, the tidy squares of farmland, and the rippling, gray-gold grasslands. The train crossed trestles and bridges and passed towns that all began to look alike to Frances. Occasionally she'd wonder if this type of farm or that kind of house would be like the one where she'd live. Sometimes she'd just sit back, her arm around Petey, and let herself be rocked by the steady rhythm of the rackety wheels that clattered over and over, "New life, new life, new life."

"But I don't want a new life," Frances murmured to herself.

"Mike and I are going to be together," Danny came to tell Frances.

Terror showed in his eyes though, and Frances said what she knew he wanted to hear: "There's a very good chance you will be."

"The people who adopt the children—are most of them kind, do you think?" Megan whispered so softly that Frances could hardly hear her.

"I'm sure they are," Frances said. "Why else would they come?"

"That's a good question," Mike said, "and I haven't found an answer to it yet. Just why would anyone want us?"

Frances put on a brave face and even managed a laugh. "Because we're a fine lot, we are, and those who get us will be lucky! That's why!"

For the moment they were content, but Frances's heart ached as she realized her words meant nothing. If she was saying only what they wanted to hear, was that what Katherine and Andrew were doing, too?

Days became nights, and nights broke into early daylights with passengers so stiff they grimaced as they stretched their legs and rubbed their arms and necks. The children and the other passengers dozed, ate, and talked. Occasionally conversation in the car grew lively, especially when the topic turned to politics and the pros and cons of slavery. Frances listened and soaked up the words when someone echoed what Da had told her.

The children changed to another train in the massive Chicago railroad station. This one would take them to the Mississippi River, where they'd cross over, heading toward Hannibal, Missouri.

Missouri! Frances would be glad to see the long train ride end, but her hands grew damp and she found it hard to breathe whenever she thought about what might await her and her brothers and sisters in St. Joseph.

The car in which they rode southwest toward Hannibal looked much the same as the first one. Outside the city, even the farms and houses looked like those they had seen for so many days, and most of the passengers on their car were the same. Frances knew that everyone was as exhausted as she was, even the adults. She remembered the flounces and parasols and grand top hats the ladies and gentlemen wore when they got on the first train in Albany. Now their once-elegant suit coats and wide, bustled dresses were wilted and dusty.

When Petey put his mouth to Frances's ear and whispered loudly, "Some of the people stink," Frances could only nod in agreement.

Mike and another boy got into a shoving match in the aisle, and Frances found herself scolding Mike with an overly sharp tongue. Mike snapped back, rudely sticking out his tongue, and it was all she could do not to slap him.

Arguments exploded among all the children as quickly and often as sparks from a burning, sap-filled log. Tousled and rumpled, Peg and Danny poked at each other unmercifully, and Petey cried over every little thing. Even Megan, who was usually gentle and even-tempered, huddled into a miserable heap next to the window.

Early one evening they reached the broad Mississippi River, which they would cross by steamboat. Standing with the others who clustered at the rail of the big paddle wheeler, Frances begged, "Please, could we stay outside to watch?"

"It's cold and damp," Katherine said. She touched Frances's cheek. "You'll be soaked by the mist rising from the water."

"We don't mind," Frances said. "It's such a big river, and so many, many boats!"

Jim stepped up beside her. "Please?" he echoed. "We want to see it all!"

Katherine laughingly agreed, but while most of the children ran up and down the deck, Jim pointed out some of the types of boats to Frances.

"I'm going to work on a boat," he said. "Maybe one of those big steamboats with twin stacks." His voice filled with yearning as he added, "Maybe a captain and his wife will adopt me."

He continued to lean on the rail, eagerly studying the heavy river traffic. But Frances soon lost interest in the boats and kept an eye on the Missouri shore ahead, watching it appear from the mists as they grew nearer.

When they arrived in Hannibal, Missouri, many passengers left to journey to St. Louis, and other passengers joined them on a third train.

We're actually in Missouri, Frances thought, and she couldn't eat a bite of the food that Andrew had brought on board for their supper.

Although Danny gobbled down his meal, Mike's appetite seemed to have disappeared, too. Frances glanced at Mike just as he looked up at her, and she knew that he shared her terror of what they might have to face when they reached St. Joseph.

"Frances," he said, then quickly corrected himself. "Frankie, I'm sorry about all this. I know that being sent west has been awful hard on you, what with you and Ma so close."

Frances quickly shook her head. "We don't have to talk about it."

"But I want to, because it's my fault that all the rest of you are here, and I'm sorry I did this to you."

"Oh, Mike." Frances reached out to touch her brother's hand. "I don't blame you." She tried to make her voice light. "Look at it this way. You kept telling me I'd like living in the West. Now I'll have a chance to find out."

But Mike didn't respond to her attempt at humor. "This is our last time to be together. After we're placed, who knows when we'll see each other again?"

"We may not know when we'll be together again, but I'm sure that we will be. I'll write to you. Will you write back?"

Mike nodded. "Sure. And someday—"

But the train squealed to such a sudden stop that they were thrown off-balance.

"Outlaws!" a woman screamed as a heavily bearded man burst through the door to their car, waving a rifle at the passengers.

Shrieks and yells came from the other cars as men on horseback galloped at each side of the train. One of the men reined in his horse and poked a long gun in through one of the open windows of the children's car.

The bearded man waved a small cloth sack at the passengers. "Sit down right now! All of you! And don't do anything we don't tell you to do," he snapped.

As she dropped back onto the bench, Frances saw Captain Taylor glance at the man on horseback outside the window and back to the outlaw in the aisle. She held her breath, wondering what he would do. But he sat quietly and kept his hand away from his satchel and his gun.

"Everybody pay attention," the outlaw demanded, little drops of spittle glittering on his beard. "Put your money and valuables in this sack." When they were slow to react he yelled, "Now!" and jabbed the end of his rifle at Mr. Crandon's stomach.

"Don't do that!" Mr. Crandon squeaked. "I'll give you all my money! See! Here it is!" He fumbled for a wad of bills held with a gleaming gold money clip and dropped it into the sack.

The outlaw moved up the aisle, thrusting the open sack ahead of him, his nervous eyes darting from one passenger to another. One by one the passengers obeyed as the outlaw eyed them closely. The women even stripped off their rings and bracelets and dropped them into the sack, and some of the men gave up their pocket watches.

As the outlaw came to Katherine she said, "I have no money."

He glanced at her hand. "You have a ring. Take it off."

"Oh, please let me keep it!" Katherine said. Frances was amazed to see tears in her eyes. "It's not of much value, but it means a great deal to me."

The man quickly glanced at the man on horseback, then back at Katherine, and his voice grew even more loud and harsh. "You heard me! Drop it in the sack! Now!"

As Katherine obeyed, the outlaw outside the window called, "Get a move on! We're ready to ride!"

Cautiously, his gun held before him, the bearded outlaw began to back away from the passengers. Suddenly Mike was in the aisle, plowing into the man, and they stumbled together as the cloth bag was almost jerked from the outlaw's hand. Angrily the man regained his balance, giving Mike such a hard clout with his left hand that he knocked him sprawling. Mike bounced off the edge of the nearest seat and landed on the floor of the car, curled facedown, not moving.

Frances gasped and rushed toward Mike as the outlaw jumped from the car.

She could hear more yelling and the sound of galloping horses as he and the rest of his gang raced away from the train. The sound of gunshots exploded outside the window, and Captain Taylor shouted, "Got one of them! But just in the shoulder, blast it!"

"Mike! Wake up!" Frances begged as she threw her arms around him. Danny dove in next to her, and in the next minute Andrew and Katherine were beside her, ready to help. But Mike squirmed away from Frances, struggled to his knees,

and stood up, one fist clenched against his chest.

Frances scrambled to her feet, too, trying once more to put her arms around her brother. "Oh, Mike! Are you hurt?"

Mike pulled away to face all the other staring passengers. Frances could see him try to smile, but tears filled his eyes.

"I was a copper stealer once." Mike's voice was barely a whisper. "I promised Ma and I promised myself that I would never pick pockets again, but I couldn't let that outlaw take Mrs. Banks's ring, not when it meant so much to her."

He held out his fist and dropped the ring into Katherine's hand.

"Oh!" Katherine gasped. "Oh, Mike!" She held the ring up to stare at it as though she couldn't believe it was really there, and tears came to her eyes, too. Quickly she bent to wrap Mike in a hug.

Around them people murmured, "How did he manage that?" "What did that boy do?"

"There's more," Mike mumbled against Katherine's shoulder. When she stepped back he held out his hand, palm up, and opened his fingers. In it lay a wad of bills. As everyone stared, Mike gave the lot to Andrew. "I couldn't get it all," he apologized, "but maybe those who lost their money could divide this."

"Good, good!" Mr. Crandon stretched to see, then scowled. "What's this! What about me? He didn't retrieve my gold money clip!"

One of the women began to chirp like a frightened bird. "The bag will be almost empty! What if that outlaw notices and comes back?"

Mike shook his head. "He won't notice. I dropped my book in the bag to give it weight." He managed a shaky grin. "The tales in those novels about brave, daring outlaws are wrong. There wasn't anything grand about that man. He was dirty and fat and smelled like a New York gutter in summer."

Katherine put an arm around Mike's shoulders, hugging him again. "You risked your life!" she said. "You shouldn't have done that." As Mike ducked his head Katherine slipped the ring back onto her finger and added quickly, "But oh, Mike, my friend, I thank you with all my heart for retrieving my ring."

Captain Taylor stepped forward to shake Mike's hand. "You exhibited great courage," he said. "I'm proud of you."

Mr. Crandon's booming voice almost [obscured]
heard that boy. He admitted to being a [obscured]

"Just a minute, Mr. Crandon!" Kath[obscured]
life during the fire."

But Mr. Crandon sputtered, "Sav[obscured]
he ruined my trousers!"

"You're not being fair to Mike! [obscured]
save some of our property."

"He tried to help!" Danny ec[obscured]

Mr. Crandon wrinkled his nose as thoug[obscured]
"Granted, the boy thought he was doing right," he said. "I'll gi[obscured] [obscured]ut
don't you see? It simply proves my point. He's never learned the right valu[es.]

"That's not true!" Frances exclaimed, but Mr. Crandon ignored her.

"A boy like that should not be allowed in a proper home! And I'll do my best
to see to it that he isn't!"

"Mr. Crandon—" Andrew began.

But a woman who had boarded the train at Hannibal raised her voice to shout
over his. "I agree. Perhaps the boy could be sent back to New York."

Her companion clutched the lapels of her jacket together as though Mike had
plans to steal it and stammered, "I think Mr. Crandon should take steps to see this
is done. We don't need a New York pickpocket here!"

"No!" Frances could stay quiet no longer. She stepped in front of Mike and
faced the surprised passengers.

"In New York," she said, "we worked very hard, but we didn't always have
enough to eat. And we didn't have clean, fine clothes like those we're wearing now.
And we didn't have our father. Da died last year. Mike was wrong to steal, but he
thought he had to so that he could bring home a bit of meat now and then. He
tried in his own way to help."

She took a long breath and hurried on before she could lose what little
courage she had left. "We're people just like you, who have the same feelings
you have."

The woman who earlier had spoken up for the children held out a hand, as

Mr. crandon doesn't trust Mike 'cause he thinks Mike will pick pocket everybody

though she were reaching for Frances, and said, "Oh, my dear child, it's plain that some of us have forgotten that you had no parents to guide you."

"We have a parent. We have a mother," Frances said, "and she and Da taught us, over and over again, the rules we should follow."

"You have a mother? But where is she?"

Frances held her chin up, willing it to stop trembling. "She sent us west," she said, trying to repeat Ma's words without thinking about them, "because she wanted us to have better lives than she could give us."

Without another word the passengers drifted back to their seats. The children, subdued and silent now, sat clustered together on the benches.

Andrew squeezed into the seat next to Frances. "Well spoken, son," he said. "I think you and Mike will do very well for yourselves in the West."

Frances glanced back at Mr. Crandon. She couldn't help being afraid, not just for Mike, but for all of them. Every minute was taking them closer to St. Joseph, to the place she had never seen that might be her home for the rest of her life. What would happen to them then?

Joan Lowery Nixon

Editor Ilene Cooper talks to Joan Lowery Nixon about her Orphan Train series:

ILENE COOPER: Where did you get your idea for *A Family Apart* and the other Orphan Train books?

JOAN LOWERY NIXON: I got it from a friend. He had read a piece in a history magazine about the Orphan Train children, and he sent it on to me. The idea excited me.

COOPER: You must have done a lot of research.

NIXON: The first thing I did was go to New York and meet with the people at the Children's Aid Society. It was the Aid Society that sent the children west. They paid for the tickets, collected clothing, advertised that they'd be coming, and paid guardians to take the children west. The Society lent me journals from the 1800s that told about the Orphan Train. The books were so old that I was almost afraid to handle them. Then I began to collect other records, such as diaries written by the Orphan Train riders themselves.

COOPER: Were most of the children true orphans, or did they, like the Kelly children, have a parent?

NIXON: Most were true orphans, but there were many immigrant children who came from one-parent homes. The parents were working long hours, and they couldn't take care of their children. The children were out on the streets and getting into trouble. Like Mrs. Kelly in the book, these parents decided their children would be better off getting out of the slums.

COOPER: You write all kinds of books—historical novels, mysteries, even picture books. How do you decide what you're going to write next?

NIXON: I look for ideas constantly. I keep a pocket file of them. I have more story ideas than I could ever possibly write. Each year I know I'm going to be writing one mystery, so everything else must fit around that.

COOPER: Are there going to be more Orphan Train books?

NIXON: Yes. There was a great response to the first four. Many readers wrote and asked me what happened next to the Kelly children. So now there are two more books. *A Dangerous Promise* is set in 1861 and is all about Mike. The next book is set in 1863 and is about Peg, who becomes a spy during the Civil War.

WESTERN

THE FORTY-NINERS
Oscar E. Berninghaus

WAGONS

BY ROSEMARY AND STEPHEN VINCENT BENÉT

They went with axe and rifle, when the trail was still to blaze
They went with wife and children, in the prairie-schooner days
With banjo and with frying pan—Susanna, don't you cry!
For I'm off to California to get rich out there or die!

We've broken land and cleared it, but we're tired of where we are.
They say that wild Nebraska is a better place by far.
There's gold in far Wyoming, there's black earth in Ioway,
So pack up the kids and blankets, for we're moving out today.

The cowards never started and the weak died on the road,
And all across the continent the endless campfires glowed
We'd taken land and settled—but a traveler passed by—
And we're going West tomorrow—Lordy, never ask us why!

We're going West tomorrow, where the promises can't fail.
O'er the hills in legions, boys, and crowd the dusty trail!
We shall starve and freeze and suffer. We shall die, and tame the lands.
But we're going West tomorrow, with our fortune in our hands.

RESPONSE CORNER

FIRE POWER

When the brushfire broke out and Mr. Crandon's shirt caught fire, Mike knew just what to do. How much do you know about fire safety? Research some tips and create a pamphlet with rules for what to do in case of fire. Make your pamphlet available to your family members.

WESTWARD HO!

Many settlers traveled west by covered wagon. The Kelly children traveled west by train and steamboat. Think about two forms of travel you have tried. Write one paragraph that compares them and one paragraph that contrasts them.

LESSONS LEARNED

Frances Kelly and her brothers and sisters learned a lot in "the classroom of life." Talk with a group of classmates about the kinds of lessons people learn inside and outside of the classroom. Share at least one lesson you have learned in each setting.

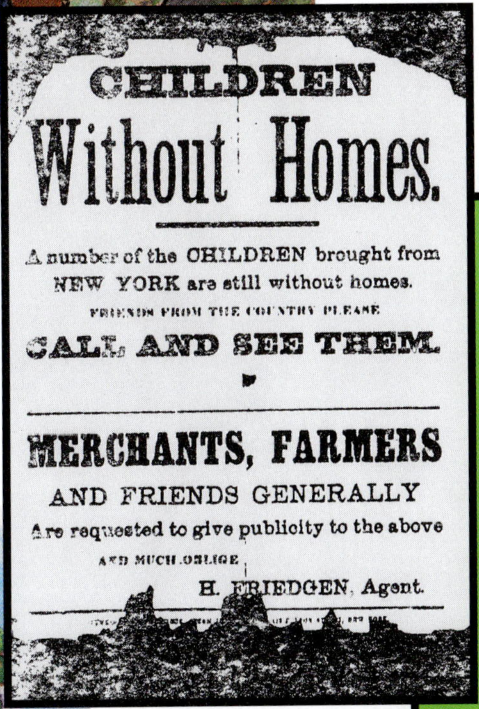

CHILDREN Without Homes.

A number of the CHILDREN brought from NEW YORK are still without homes.
FRIENDS FROM THE COUNTRY PLEASE

CALL AND SEE THEM.

MERCHANTS, FARMERS

AND FRIENDS GENERALLY

Are requested to give publicity to the above
AND MUCH OBLIGE

H. FRIEDGEN, Agent.

WHAT DO YOU THINK?

- What kind of person is Frances? Mike? Give examples from the story that show their personality traits.

- If you could be one of the characters in the story, who would you choose to be? Explain your choice.

- How are the Kelly children like the settlers described in the poem "Western Wagons"? How are they different?

577

HECTOR

LIVES IN THE UNITED STATES NOW

THE STORY OF A
MEXICAN-AMERICAN CHILD
by Joan Hewett
Photographs by Richard Hewett

Ten-year-old Hector Almaraz is a

Mexican American. For as long as he can

remember he has lived in Los Angeles—

in this neighborhood, on this block.

Hector's parents are Leopoldo and

Rosario Almaraz. He also has three

brothers: nine-year-old Polo, and Miguel

and Ernesto, who are seven and four.

Notable Trade
Book in the Field
of Social Studies

Hector and Polo were born in Guadalajara, Mexico, and are Mexican citizens, like their parents. Their younger brothers, Miguel and Ernesto, were born in Los Angeles and are American citizens.

When Hector's parents came to California to find work, they did not understand English. But they had heard so much about Los Angeles, from sisters and brothers and their own parents, that the city seemed almost familiar.

At first they stayed with relatives. Then Leopoldo found a job, and the family moved to Eagle Rock, a residential section of the city.

They are still there. The streets and parks are safe, and an elementary school and a Catholic church are only a few blocks from their small, bungalow-style apartment.

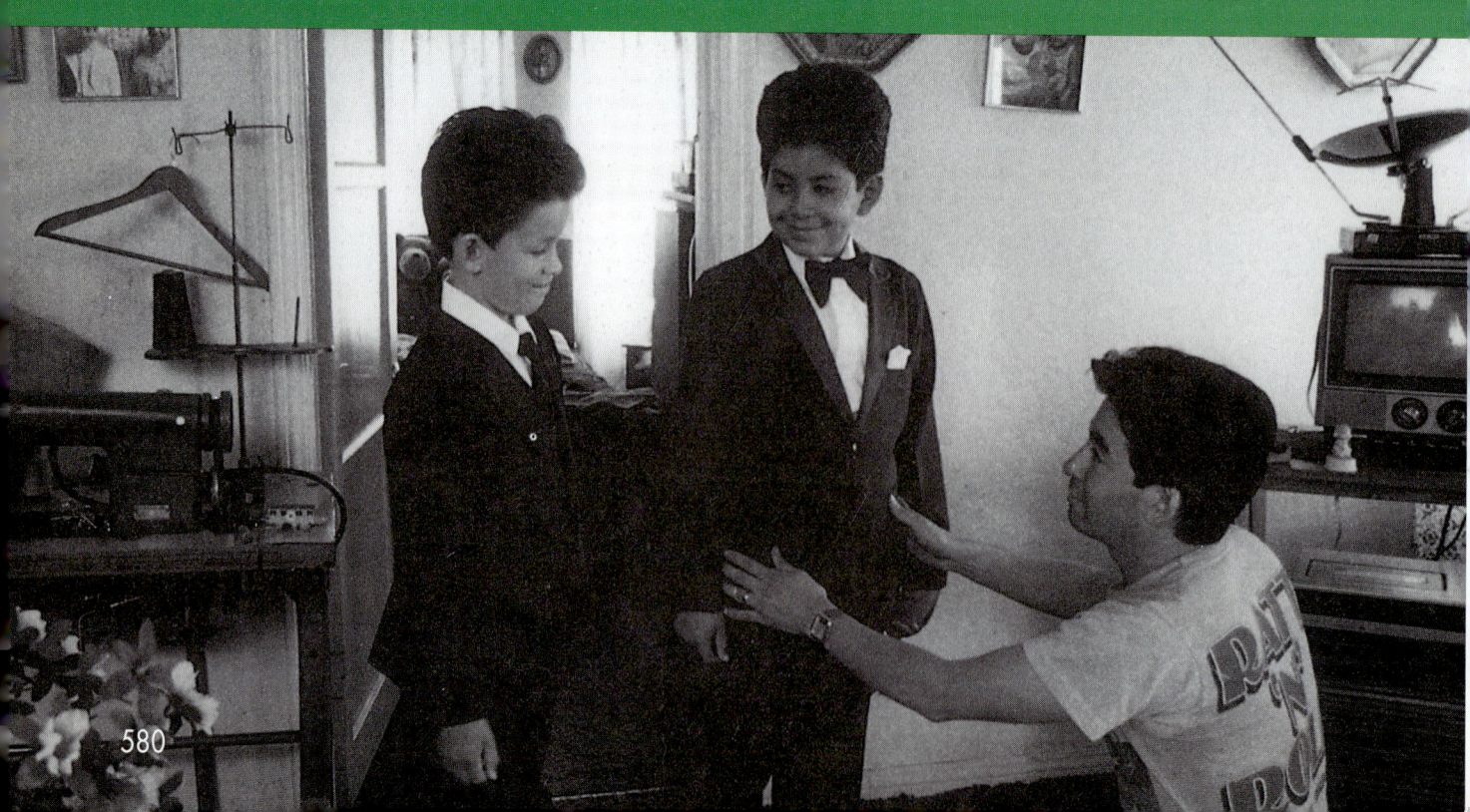

Hector has lots of friends. Most of them live on his block. They play together after school and on Saturdays and Sundays.

Soccer is one of their favorite games. So is baseball. When it is baseball season, they dig out a bat, ball, and glove and practice batting in a backyard or alley. Other times they go to the park to play volleyball, or just to see what is going on. If no one has a flat, they ride their bikes over; otherwise they walk.

Like his friends, Hector likes to read comic books and collect baseball cards. Sometimes they gather their cards or books, meet on the front stoop, and trade. Although the children talk and joke in English, their parents come from Mexico and Central America, and Spanish is the language spoken in their homes.

When Hector and Polo are drawing or doing their homework at the kitchen table, they often tell stories to each other in English. They speak as fast as they can so their mother will not understand them. Rosario gets annoyed because she suspects they do it just to tease her.

Although Hector and Polo speak English equally well, their parents think it proper that their eldest boy be the family spokesperson. Hector enjoys the responsibility. Whenever someone who can only speak English telephones them, Hector is called to the phone. Or when Rosario has to get a prescription filled at the drugstore, Hector goes along to talk to the pharmacist.

Hector did not speak English when he started kindergarten. It was a scary time. He was away from his mother and brothers. He understood only a few English words and did not know what was going on in class. In first grade Hector had trouble learning to read. But he was determined to learn English, and by the end of the second grade he was reading and writing as well as his classmates. School started to be fun.

Now Hector is a fifth grader, one of the big kids. In United States history, his class is reading about the different immigrant groups who helped settle the West. Their teacher says, "We are a nation of immigrants. Indians, also called Native Americans, have lived here for thousands of years. Everyone else has come to the continental United States from some other place." Then she smiles and says, "Let's find out about us."

The students in Hector's class are told to ask their parents about their ancestors and then write a brief history of their families. It is an exciting project. When they finish their reports, they will glue snapshots of themselves to their papers and hang them on the wall. But first they get to read them aloud.

Philip traces his family back as far as his great-great-great-grandmother. His ancestors lived on a small Philippine island. Many of them were fishermen. Philip, his sister, and his parents are the only people in his family who have settled in the United States.

One side of Nicky's family came from Norway and Germany. His other ancestors came from Ireland and Sweden. All of them were farmers, and when they came to this country they homesteaded land, which means they farmed and built a house on uncultivated public land that then became theirs under a special homestead law.

Vanessa's great-great-grandmother was a Yaqui Indian from Sonora, Mexico. Her grandfather fought in the Mexican Revolution. Another one of her ancestors was French.

Erick is descended from Ukrainian, German, and Italian immigrants. His German grandfather and Ukrainian grandmother met in a prisoner-of-war camp. When they were released, they married and came to the United States by ship.

Julie is of French, Irish, and Spanish descent. Her Great-Great-Grandma Elm was born in Texas. When Elm was a child her family moved to California. They traveled by covered wagon.

Everyone is interested in Kyria's family history. One of her African ancestors was a soldier in the American Revolution. Another fought for the Confederacy in the Civil War. Other members of her family homesteaded in Oklahoma.

Hector tells the class about his Mexican ancestors. They were farmers and carpenters.

There are twelve other Mexican-American children in Hector's class, and some two hundred fifty thousand Mexican-American students in Los Angeles schools.

Before California became part of the United States, it belonged to Mexico. Some Mexican families have lived in California for hundreds of years, but most Mexican-American children are recent arrivals. Their numbers will keep increasing.

Compared to the United States, Mexico is not a prosperous country, and in the last few years Mexico's economy has declined sharply. More than half its workers cannot find jobs. So, many go north to look for jobs on the other side of the Mexican-American border, a 1,900-mile boundary that separates California, Arizona, New Mexico, and Texas from Mexico.

Some Mexicans are among the six hundred thousand immigrants from all over the world who are granted permanent residence in the United States each year.

DREAM
America

illustrated by Guy Porfirio

George Washington
helped get the Dream started—
praise and honor to him—
But he couldn't finish dreaming it for us.
No one can finish dreaming the Dream.

Abraham Lincoln
helped shape the Dream—
praise and honor to him—
But he couldn't finish dreaming it for us.
No one can finish dreaming the Dream.

Great men and women
can help us to dream—
praise and honor to them—
But they can't dream it all up for us.
The Dream of America must be our Dream.

—*Juan Quintana*

RESPONSE

CALCULATE DISTANCES

ACROSS MANY BORDERS

Locate Guadalajara, Mexico, on a map of North America. Find the distance between Guadalajara and Los Angeles. Then figure out the distances immigrants from several other parts of the world would have to travel to reach other parts of America.

ROLE-PLAY

TIPS FROM THE AUTHOR

Hector learned how to speak English in order to succeed in school. Suppose you were tutoring another person in English. What important tips would you share? Role-play the tutoring session with a partner. Then switch roles.

CORNER

THE AMERICAN DREAM

The United States is "a nation of immigrants." Almost all of us, or our families, have come to America in search of a dream. Find out from which country or countries your family came. Share this family history, and a glimpse of your American dream, in an information paragraph.

WHAT DO YOU THINK?

• What do you think Hector's teacher means when she says, "We are a nation of immigrants"?

• How would you feel if you, like Hector, had to move to a new country and learn a new language?

• How have the families of Hector and his classmates taken part in the American Dream described in "Dream America"?

591

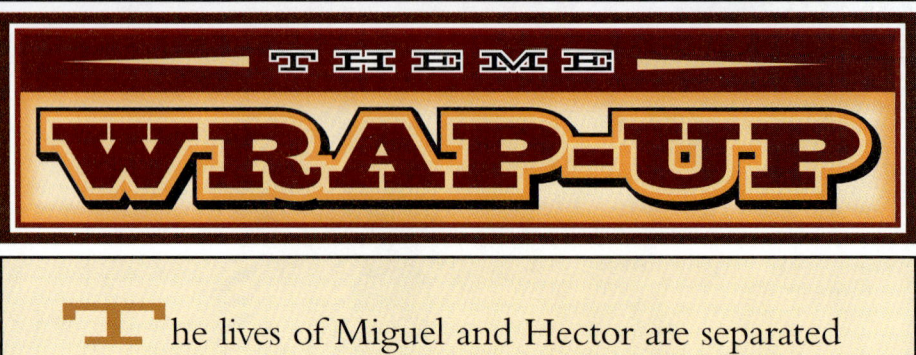

The lives of Miguel and Hector are separated by 400 years. What can you think of that they might have in common?

Of all the children in this theme, who seems best suited to adapt to a new life in a new land? Why?

ACTIVITY CORNER

Imagine that, like the children in this theme, you became a pioneer in a strange new world. Imagine that your new world was on a new planet. Describe and name your new planet, and tell about some of its beauties and dangers.

Glossary

WHAT IS A GLOSSARY?

A glossary is like a small dictionary at the back of a book. It lists some of the words used in the book, along with their pronunciations, their meanings, and other useful information. If you come across a word you don't know as you are reading, you can look up the word in this glossary.

Using the

Like a dictionary, this glossary lists words in alphabetical order. To find a word, look it up by its first letter or letters.

To save time, use the **guide words** at the top of each page. These show you the first and last words on the page. Look at the guide words to see if your word falls between them alphabetically.

Here is an example of a glossary entry:

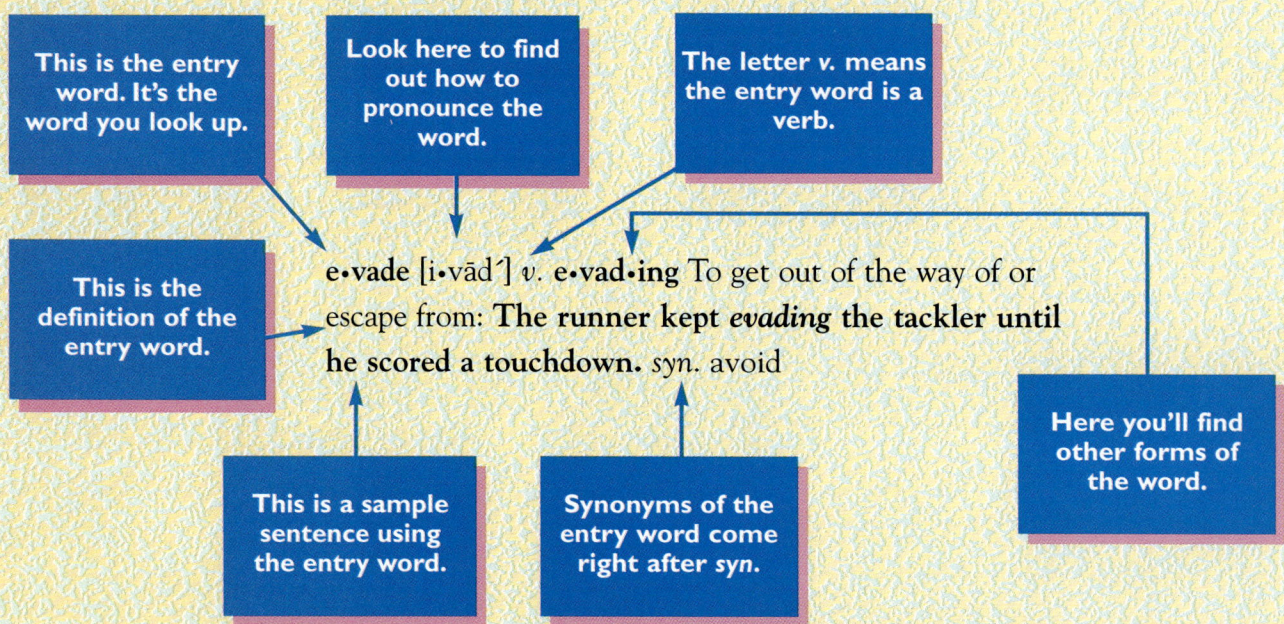

This is the entry word. It's the word you look up.

Look here to find out how to pronounce the word.

The letter *v.* means the entry word is a verb.

This is the definition of the entry word.

e•vade [i•vād´] *v.* e•vad•ing To get out of the way of or escape from: **The runner kept** *evading* **the tackler until he scored a touchdown.** *syn.* avoid

This is a sample sentence using the entry word.

Synonyms of the entry word come right after *syn.*

Here you'll find other forms of the word.

ETYMOLOGY

Etymology is the study or history of how words are developed. Words often have interesting backgrounds that can help you remember what they mean. Look in the margins of the glossary to find the etymologies of certain words.

Here is an example of an etymology:

transmission   In Latin, *transire* means to "go across" and *mittere* means "to send." Today, transmissions can go not only across oceans but also across the galaxy.

Glossary

PRONUNCIATION

The pronunciation in brackets is a respelling that shows how the word is pronounced.

The **pronunciation key** explains what the symbols in a respelling mean. A shortened pronunciation key appears on every other page of the glossary.

- • separates words into syllables
- ´ indicates heavy stress on a syllable
- ´ indicates lighter stress on a syllable

PRONUNCIATION KEY*

a	add, map	m	move, seem	u	up, done
ā	ace, rate	n	nice, tin	û(r)	burn, term
â(r)	care, air	ng	ring, song	yo͞o	fuse, few
ä	palm, father	o	odd, hot	v	vain, eve
b	bat, rub	ō	open, so	w	win, away
ch	check, catch	ô	order, jaw	y	yet, yearn
d	dog, rod	oi	oil, boy	z	zest, muse
e	end, pet	ou	pout, now	zh	vision, pleasure
ē	equal, tree	o͝o	took, full	ə	the schwa, an
f	fit, half	o͞o	pool, food		unstressed vowel
g	go, log	p	pit, stop		representing the
h	hope, hate	r	run, poor		sound spelled
i	it, give	s	see, pass		a in *above*
ī	ice, write	sh	sure, rush		e in *sicken*
j	joy, ledge	t	talk, sit		i in *possible*
k	cool, take	th	thin, both		o in *melon*
l	look, rule	͟th	this, bathe		u in *circus*

Abbreviations: *adj.* adjective, *adv.* adverb, *conj.* conjunction, *interj.* interjection, *n.* noun, *prep.* preposition, *pron.* pronoun, *syn.* synonym, *v.* verb.

*The Pronunciation Key, adapted entries, and the Short Key that appear on the following pages are reprinted from *HBJ School Dictionary* Copyright © 1990 by Harcourt Brace & Company. Reprinted by permission of Harcourt Brace & Company.

adobe This word comes from the Spanish word *adobar*, which means "to plaster."

adobe

aviator Either a man or a woman may be called an *aviator*. The words *aviatrix* and *aviatress*, formerly used for a woman aviator, are no longer used.

broadcaster

A

a·bate [ə•bāt´] *v.* **a·bat·ed** To become less: **After it rained for two days, the storm *abated*.**

a·ble-bod·ied [ā´bəl•bod´ēd] *adj.* Strong and healthy; fit.

ab·o·li·tion·ist [ab´ə•lish´ə•nist] *adj.* Wanting to end slavery in the United States: **Many *abolitionist* groups helped slaves escape to freedom.**

ac·com·plish·ment [ə•kom´plish•mənt] *n.* Something finished successfully: **Reading ten books is a great *accomplishment*.**

ad·dress [ə•dres´] *n.* A speech: **President Lincoln's most famous speech is called the Gettysburg *Address*.**

ad·journ [ə•jûrn´] *v.* **ad·journed** To end a meeting: **The student council president *adjourned* the meeting at 3:30 P.M.**

a·do·be [ə•dō´bē] *adj.* Made of sun-dried clay bricks: ***Adobe* buildings can be found in the southwestern United States.**

al·ma·nac [ôl´mə•nak] *n.* **al·ma·nacs** A book that has facts about the seasons, the heavens, and other information and features: **Some farmers look in *almanacs* to find out when to plant crops.**

an·ces·tor [an´ses•tər] *n.* **an·ces·tors** Someone in a family who lived a long time ago: **Rasheed's *ancestors* were from India.**

anx·ious·ly [angk´shəs•lē] *adv.* Nervously: **José waited *anxiously* to see the dentist.**

ap·pre·ci·ate [ə•prē´shē•āt´] *v.* **ap·pre·ci·at·ed** To value: **Your full cooperation is *appreciated*.**

as·tron·o·my [ə•stron´ə•mē] *n.* The study of stars and planets: ***Astronomy* was Maria's favorite class.**

a·vi·a·tor [ā´vē•ā´tər] *n.* A person who flies an airplane. *syn.* pilot

B

bar·i·tone [bar´ə•tōn´] *n.* A male with a medium-range singing voice: **The main singer in the opera was a *baritone*.**

black·mail [blak´māl´] *v.* To force someone to pay to keep a secret: **Someone tried to *blackmail* Simon about cheating on his test.**

bol·ster [bōl´•stər] *v.* To make stronger: **Billy ran daily to *bolster* his strength for the race.**

broad·cast·er [brôd´kas•tər] *n.* A radio or television announcer.

C

cam·pus [kam′pəs] *n.* The grounds of a school or college: **The students could not leave** *campus* **during the day.**

cit·i·zen [sit′ə·zən] *n.* **cit·i·zens** A person who is born in or made a member of a city or country.

com·mem·o·rate [kə·mem′ə·rāt′] *v.* **com·mem·o·rat·ed** To remember with honor: **The parade** *commemorated* **the end of the war.**

com·mu·nal [kom′yə·nəl or kə·myōo′nəl] *adj.* Owned and used by a group of people: **Winston works in a** *communal* **garden.**

com·pe·tent·ly [kom′pə·tənt·lē] *adv.* Skillfully: **Diane** *competently* **pulled the fish out of the water.**

com·pul·so·ry [kəm·pul′sər·ē] *adj.* Having to be done: **Training in CPR is** *compulsory for all new lifeguards.* *syn.* required

con·coc·tion [kən·kok′shən or kon·kok′shən] *n.* Something made by mixing things together: **Susan made her special** *concoction,* **a strawberry-chocolate shake.**

con·demned [kən·demd′] *adj.* Marked as unsafe for use: **The** *condemned* **building was torn down.**

con·ser·va·tion [kon′sər·vā′shən] *n.* The careful use and protection of natural resources: **When water is scarce, we must practice** *conservation.*

co·op·er·a·tive [kō·op′rə·tiv] *n.* Something owned and run by a group of people: **Benjie and Kim live in a housing** *cooperative.*

cringe [krinj] *v.* To move back in fear: **The buzzing bee made her** *cringe.*

cul·prit [kul′prit] *n.* Someone who is guilty of doing something wrong.

cul·ti·vat·ed [kul′tə·vāt′ed] *adj.* Made ready to grow plants: **Zach planted seeds in the** *cultivated* **garden.**

D

dem·on·stra·tion [dem′ən·strā′shən] *n.* A showing of how something works: **I saw a** *demonstration* **of the new computer.**

de·prive [di·prīv′] *v.* **de·priv·ing** To keep from having: **Andre is** *depriving* **himself of candy.**

des·o·late [des′ə·lit] *adj.* Without people; barren: **The old farm stood empty and** *desolate.*

di·a·lect [dī′ə·lekt′] *n.* The way a language is spoken in one part of a country: **The** *dialect* **my grandparents speak is different from mine.**

dire [dīr] *adj.* Terrible; extreme: **The flood left us in** *dire* **need of help.**

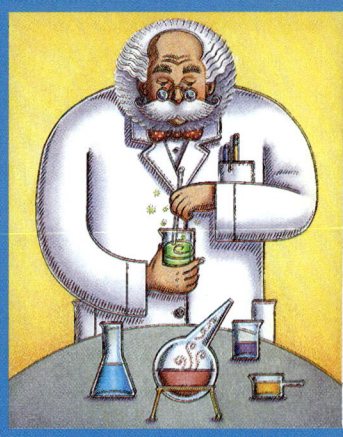

dire

concoction

desolate

a	add	o͝o	took
ā	ace	o͞o	pool
â	care	u	up
ä	palm	û	burn
e	end	yo͞o	fuse
ē	equal	oi	oil
i	it	ou	pout
ī	ice	ng	ring
o	odd	th	thin
ō	open	ŧ͟h	this
ô	order	zh	vision

$$ə = \begin{cases} \text{a in } above \\ \text{e in } sicken \\ \text{i in } possible \\ \text{o in } melon \\ \text{u in } circus \end{cases}$$

eccentricity

Although *eccentricities* may make you the center of attention, this word comes from the Latin words *ex* and *centros*, meaning "out from the center." The center was the normal place to be, so if people were not in the center, they were considered different and strange.

eclipse

edition

dis·mal [diz´məl] *adj.* Sad or gloomy: **Because the weather was *dismal*, we stayed home.**

dis·tri·bu·tion [dis´trə·byo͞o´shən] *n.* The arrangement of something in space or time: **The scientist is studying the *distribution* of plants on the hillside.**

do·na·tion [dō·nā´shən] *n.* A gift, usually to a good cause. *syn.* contribution

dread·ful [dred´fəl] *adj.* Awful: **The old piano sounded *dreadful*.** *syn.* terrible

ec·cen·tric·i·ty [ek´sen·tris´ə·tē] *n.* **ec·cen·tric·i·ties** A behavior that is odd: **The children thought the man's *eccentricities* were fascinating.**

e·clipse [i·klips´] *n.* **e·clips·es** A complete or partial hiding of the sun or of the moon.

e·co·sys·tem [ek´ō·sis´təm] *n.* **e·co·sys·tems** The relationship of plants, animals, and people in an area to their environment and to each other: **There are several *ecosystems* in the rain forest.**

e·di·tion [i·dish´ən] *n.* All the copies of a book printed at one time: **When the first *edition* sold out, they printed a second *edition*.**

em·pha·size [em´fə·sīz´] *v.* **em·pha·siz·es** To point out in a special way: **The teacher *emphasizes* that we should be in class on time.**

en·sem·ble [än·säm´bəl] *n.* A group that performs together: **There were four horns in the brass *ensemble*.**

en·ti·tle [in·tīt´(ə)l] *v.* **en·ti·tled** To give the right to do something: **Because she had finished her work, Cara was *entitled* to go to the gym.**

es·tab·lish [i·stab´lish] *v.* To set up: **The Pilgrims came to America to *establish* settlements.**

e·vade [i·vād´] *v.* **e·vad·ing** To get out of the way of or escape from: **The runner kept *evading* tacklers until he scored a touchdown.** *syn.* avoid

ex·clu·sive·ly [iks·klo͞o´siv·lē] *adv.* Only: **The picnic was *exclusively* for fifth graders.**

flus·ter [flus´tər] *v.* **flus·tered** To confuse or upset: **Celia was *flustered* when she was asked to sing for the class.**

for·feit [fôr´fit] *v.* **for·feit·ed** To give something up, as a penalty: **The team *forfeited* the championship because of cheating.**

for·mal [fôr´məl] *adj.* Following set rules or patterns; regular: **My grandmother had only six years of *formal* schooling.**

found [found] *v.* **found·ed** To start or set up: **The Spanish *founded* many missions in North America.**

G

grov·el [gruv´əl or grov´əl] *v.* **grov·el·ing** To crawl in fear with the face downward: **The people were *groveling* before the king because they feared his power.**

H

ham·mock [ham´ək] *n.* A long piece of strong cloth hung up by its ends to lie in.

har·vest [här´vist] *v.* To bring in a crop: **It is time to *harvest* the corn.** *syn.* pick

I

im·mi·grant [im´ə·grənt] *n.* A person who moves to another country to live.

im·pact [im´pakt] *n.* A strong effect: **The computer has a great *impact* on our lives.**

im·pose [im·pōz´] *v.* To force: **Roberto's parents wanted to *impose* a 9:00 P.M. bedtime on him.**

in·di·cate [in´də·kāt´] *v.* To show or give a sign of: **The signs above the doors *indicate* the exits.**

in·dus·tri·ous [in·dus´trē·əs] *adj.* Hardworking: **Ants are *industrious* insects.**

in·flu·ence [in´floo·əns] *n.* Power over someone's thoughts or actions without using force: **Sandra was a good *influence* on her younger sister.**

in·gen·ious [in·jēn´yəs] *adj.* Skillful and clever: **Her *ingenious* project won first prize.**

in·hab·it [in·hab´it] *v.* To live in: **Dolphins *inhabit* the oceans.**

in·quir·y [in·kwīr´ē or in´kwər·ē] *n.* **in·quir·ies** An attempt to find out information: **Aunt Shirley made *inquiries* about my mother's health.**

in·to·na·tion [in´tō·nā´shən] *n.* The ability to play or sing a note in tune: **Violet has excellent *intonation* when she sings.**

in·vis·i·ble [in·viz´ə·bəl] *adj.* Not able to be seen: **An *invisible* force field protected the spaceship.**

ir·ri·ga·tion [ir´ə·gā´shən] *n.* The bringing of water to dry land: **The farmers need *irrigation* to grow crops in the desert.**

irrigation

hammock

harvest

a	add	ŏŏ	took
ā	ace	ōō	pool
â	care	u	up
ä	palm	û	burn
e	end	yōō	fuse
ē	equal	oi	oil
i	it	ou	pout
ī	ice	ng	ring
o	odd	th	thin
ō	open	th	this
ô	order	zh	vision

ə = { a in *above*
e in *sicken*
i in *possible*
o in *melon*
u in *circus*

knead

K

knead [nēd] *v.* **knead•ed** To press or squeeze together: **The baker** *kneaded* **the bread dough.**

L

land•mark [land´märk´] *n.* **land•marks** An easily recognized object, such as a tree or building.

land•scape [land´skāp´] *n.* A wide view of natural scenery: **The mountain** *landscape* **was beautiful.**

laugh•ing•stock [laf´ing•stok´] *n.* A person or thing that people make fun of: **When I struck out, I was the** *laughingstock* **of my team.**

lib•er•ty [lib´ər•tē] *n.* Freedom: **Many people come to the United States to find** *liberty.*

maneuver

M

ma•neu•ver [mə•n(y)oo´vər] *v.* **ma•neu•vered** To move with skill: **Maria** *maneuvered* **the car into the parking space.**

mar•i•ner [mar´ə•nər] *n.* **mar•i•ners** A sailor.

mem•o•ra•ble [mem´ər•ə•bəl] *adj.* Hard to forget: **Ben's birthday party at the zoo was** *memorable.*

mesa

me•sa [mā´sə] *n.* **me•sas** A steep hill with a flat top: **From the tops of the** *mesas,* **the Navajos could see for miles.**

mon•soon [mon•soon´] *n.* A season of strong winds and rain in Asia: **The rains of the** *monsoon* **turned the dusty road into a river of mud.**

muf•fle [muf´əl] *v.* To wrap something in order to deaden its sound: **A pillow can** *muffle* **the sound of the radio.**

mute [myoot] *adj.* Not being able to speak: **The doll was** *mute.*

mu•ti•ny [myoo´tə•nē] *n.* Taking power from the person in charge: **The sailors planned a** *mutiny* **against the cruel captain.**

N

neu•tral•i•ty [n(y)oo•tral´ə•tē] *n.* The condition of not taking sides: **Switzerland is known for its** *neutrality* **in European wars.**

non•cha•lant [non´shə•länt´] *adj.* Not excited or concerned: **Helen was** *nonchalant* **about running in the race.**

nu•tri•ent [n(y)oo´trē•ənt] *n.* **nu•tri•ents** A food needed for life and growth: **The body needs** *nutrients* **from a variety of foods.**

O

or·a·tor [ôr´ə·tər] n. A good speech maker: **LeRoy was such a good orator that he won the speech contest.**

P

par·ti·tion [pär·tish´ən] n. A dividing wall or screen: **Our classroom has a partition between the study area and the art table.**

pe·cul·iar [pi·kyoōl´yər] adj. Strange or odd: **His old-fashioned clothes look peculiar.**

per·pet·u·ate [pər·pech´oō·āt´] v. To make something last a long time: **They put up a statue to perpetuate her memory.**

pi·e·ty [pī´ə·tē] n. The showing of respect: **Many parents want their children to learn piety.**

pneu·mo·nia [n(y)oō·mōn´yə] n. A lung disease: **Nadia got pneumonia and had to stay in the hospital.**

poul·try [pōl´trē] n. Chickens, ducks, or turkeys.

priv·i·lege [priv´ə·lij] n. **priv·i·leg·es** A special advantage: **Karen's ticket gave her extra privileges at the park.** *syn.* benefit

pro·fes·sion·al [prō·fesh´ən·əl] adj. Doing something for a living, not just for a hobby: **DeeDee wants to be a professional singer.**

pro·pel·ler [prə·pel´ər] n. Blades that spin to move a boat or an aircraft.

pros and cons [prōz and konz] n. The reasons for and against something: **Before I vote, I want to know the pros and cons of the issue.**

prose [prōz] n. Speech or writing that is not poetry: **The novel won an award for its beautiful prose.**

pros·per·ous [pros´pər·əs] adj. Wealthy or rich: **The family worked hard and became prosperous.**

pro·vi·sion [prə·vizh´ən] n. **pro·vi·sions** A supply of food: **We brought enough provisions to last five days.**

prowl [proul] v. **prowls** To move around quietly, searching for something: **The leopard prowls the land in search of food.**

Q

quar·tet [kwôr·tet´] n. A piece of music played or sung by four people: **The quartet was the second piece on the program.**

R

re·cit·al [ri·sīt´(ə)l] n. A concert or performance: **Jamal practiced hard for his piano recital.**

recital

quartet There are many words in English that come from the Latin number *quadra,* or "four," for example, *quarter* and *quart.*

propeller

provisions

a	add	o͝o	took
ā	ace	o͞o	pool
â	care	u	up
ä	palm	û	burn
e	end	yo͞o	fuse
ē	equal	oi	oil
i	it	ou	pout
ī	ice	ng	ring
o	odd	th	thin
ō	open	t͟h	this
ô	order	zh	vision

$$ə = \begin{cases} \text{a in } above \\ \text{e in } sicken \\ \text{i in } possible \\ \text{o in } melon \\ \text{u in } circus \end{cases}$$

residential

spectators

symphony

reck·on [rek´ən] *v.* To guess, compute: **We** *reckon* **the trip will take a week.**

res·i·den·tial [rez´ə•den´shəl] *adj.* A place with homes, not offices or factories: **The** *residential* **part of the city is by the lake.**

res·o·lu·tion [rez´ə•loo´shən] *n.* **res·o·lu·tions** An idea to be voted upon: **The council had six** *resolutions* **to vote upon.**

res·to·ra·tion [res´tə•rā´shən] *n.* Putting things back the way they were: **The** *restoration* **of the old house took two years.**

room and board [room and bôrd] *n.* A place to sleep and food to eat: **Instead of money, Sam got** *room and board* **for working at the factory.**

S

sac·ri·fice [sak´rə•fīs´] *n.* Something that is given up as an offering: **It was a** *sacrifice* **for Joey to give the last piece of pie to his brother.**

sar·cas·ti·cal·ly [sär•kas´tik•lē] *adv.* In an unpleasant, mocking way: **"I love getting flu shots,"** she said *sarcastically.*

scale [skāl] *n.* **scales** A pattern of tones going up and down eight notes: **Flute players practice** *scales* **so they can play smoothly.**

scour [skour] *v.* **scoured** To search every part: **Dad** *scoured* **the house looking for his car keys.**

sift [sift] *v.* To sort: **The jury must** *sift* **through the evidence.**

smug·gle [smug´əl] *v.* **smug·gling** To secretly bring something into or out of a country: **The men were arrested for** *smuggling* **diamonds.**

som·ber·ly [som´bər•lē] *adv.* In a sad way: **They** *somberly* **waited for the bad news.**

spec·ta·tor [spek´tā•tər] *n.* **spec·ta·tors** A person who watches an event: **The crowd of** *spectators* **cheered loudly.**

spokes·per·son [spōks´pûr´sən] *n.* A person who speaks for another person or group of people: **The mayor is the** *spokesperson* **for our city.**

stage fright [stāj frīt] *n.* Fear of performing in public: **The actors felt** *stage fright* **before the play started.**

stat·ic [stat´ik] *n.* Electrical noise on a television or radio.

strag·gler [strag´lər] *n.* **strag·glers** A person who falls behind the main group: **The tour guide said the bus would not wait for** *stragglers.*

sym·pho·ny [sim´fə•nē] *n.* A long piece of music for an orchestra.

syn·thet·ic [sin•thet´ik] *adj.* Made by people, not by nature: **Nylon is a** *synthetic* **cloth.**

tem·po [tem´pō] *n.* The speed at which a piece of music is played.

ter·ri·to·ry [ter´ə·tôr´ē] *n.* An area of land ruled by a nation: **Puerto Rico is a *territory* of the United States.**

tol·er·ate [tol´ər·āt´] *v.* To allow: **The dog will not *tolerate* people pulling its tail.**

trans·fixed [trans·fikst´] *adj.* Frozen with shock or fear: **They watched *transfixed* as the train sped toward them.**

trans·mis·sion [trans·mish´ən] *n.* A message or program sent over TV or radio: **The police received an emergency *transmission* on their radio.**

truce [trōōs] *n.* An agreement to stop fighting for a time: **A *truce* was called to get help for those who were hurt.**

tur·bu·lence [tûr´byə·ləns] *n.* Rough and violent movement of the air: **The *turbulence* caused the plane to bounce around.**

U

un·furl [un·fûrl´] *v.* **un·furled** To unroll or unfold: **The student *unfurled* the flag.**

un·rav·el [un·rav´əl] *v.* **un·rav·el·ing** To solve: **People have spent their lives *unraveling* the mystery of the pyramids.**

up·roar [up´rôr´] *n.* Noise and confusion: **There was an *uproar* when the dog chased the cat.**

V

vague [vāg] *adj.* Not clear: **Stanley gave a *vague* explanation about why he missed school.**

veg·e·ta·tion [vej´ə·tā´shən] *n.* Plant life: **The rain forest is thick with *vegetation*.**

ves·sel [ves´(ə)l] *n.* **ves·sels** A boat or ship.

ve·to [vē´tō] *v.* **ve·toed** To not allow something to be done: **The President *vetoed* the bill that Congress sent to him.**

vi·o·late [vī´ə·lāt´] *v.* **vi·o·lat·ed** To break a rule or law: **The driver got a ticket because he *violated* the speed limit.**

vis·u·al·ize [vizh´oo·əl·īz´] *v.* To picture in the mind: **On a hot day, it helps to *visualize* a cool ocean.**

Y

yield [yēld] *v.* To produce: **I hope our tree will *yield* a lot of apples.**

transmission In Latin, *transire* means "to go across" and *mittere* means "to send." Today, *transmissions* can go not only across oceans but also across the galaxy.

vegetation

a	add	oŏ	took
ā	ace	ōō	pool
â	care	u	up
ä	palm	û	burn
e	end	yōō	fuse
ē	equal	oi	oil
i	it	ou	pout
ī	ice	ng	ring
o	odd	th	thin
ō	open	th	this
ô	order	zh	vision

ə = { a in *above*
e in *sicken*
i in *possible*
o in *melon*
u in *circus* }

INDEX OF
Titles and Authors

Page numbers in color refer to biographical information.

Printed in the United States of America

Acknowledgments

For permission to reprint copyrighted material, grateful acknowledgment is made to the following sources:

Harry N. Abrams, Inc., New York: "Fifth Grade" by Endō Mina from *Festival in My Heart: Poems by Japanese Children*, selected and translated from the Japanese by Bruno Navasky. Published by Harry N. Abrams, Inc., 1993.

Virginia Hamilton Adoff: "Under the Back Porch" by Virginia Hamilton. Text copyright © 1992, 1996 by Virginia Hamilton Adoff.

The Asia Society: "Summer" by Tran Thanh-tong from *A Thousand Years of Vietnamese Poetry*, edited by Nguyen Ngoc Bich. Text copyright © 1962, 1967, 1968, 1969, 1970, 1971, 1972, 1974 by Asia Society, Inc.

Atheneum Books for Young Readers, an imprint of Simon & Schuster: From *Shiloh* by Phyllis Reynolds Naylor. Text copyright © 1991 by Phyllis Reynolds Naylor. Cover illustration by Judith Gwyn Brown from *Maudie in the Middle* by Phyllis Reynolds Naylor. Illustration copyright © 1988 by Judith Gwyn Brown.

Avon Books: From *Sideways Stories from Wayside School* by Louis Sachar. Text copyright © 1978 by Louis Sachar.

Bantam Books, a division of Bantam Doubleday Dell Publishing Group,Inc.: From *A Family Apart* by Joan Lowery Nixon. Text copyright © 1987 by Joan Lowery Nixon and Daniel Weiss Associates, Inc.

Brandt & Brandt Literary Agents, Inc.: "Western Wagons" by Rosemary and Stephen Vincent Benét from *The Selected Works of Stephen Vincent Benét*. Text copyright 1937 by Stephen Vincent Benét; text copyright renewed © 1964 by Thomas Benét, Stephanie B. Manin and Rachel Benét Lewis. Published by Holt, Rinehart and Winston, Inc.

Carolrhoda Books, Inc., Minneapolis, MN: Cover illustration from *Song of the Chirimia* by Jane Anne Volkmer. Copyright © 1990 by Carolrhoda Books, Inc.

Children's Book Press, San Francisco, CA: "This Land Is My Land" from *This Land Is My Land* by George Littlechild. Copyright © 1993 by George Littlechild.

Children's Television Workshop: "Inventions" by Sara Jane Brian, illustrated by David Coulson from *3-2-1 Contact* Magazine, June 1995. Copyright 1995 by Children's Television Workshop.

Clarion Books, a Houghton Mifflin Company imprint: From *Children of the Wild West* by Russell Freedman. Text copyright © 1983 by Russell Freedman. Cover photograph courtesy of Chicago Historical Society from *Lincoln: A Photobiography* by Russell Freedman.

Coward-McCann, Inc., a member of The Putnam & Grosset Group: From *Where Was Patrick Henry on the 29th of May?* by Jean Fritz, illustrated by Margot Tomes. Text copyright © 1975 by Jean Fritz; illustrations copyright © 1975 by Margot Tomes. Cover illustration by Margot Tomes from *What's the Big Idea, Ben Franklin?* by Jean Fritz. Illustration copyright © 1976 by Margot Tomes.

CRICKET Magazine: From "Patchwork Quilting" by Anita Howard Wade from CRICKET Magazine, September 1995. Text copyright © 1995 by Anita Howard Wade.

Crown Publishers, Inc.: From *The Third Planet* by Sally Ride and Tam O'Shaughnessy. Copyright © 1994 by Sally Ride.

Pat Cummings: Illustration by Pat Cummings from "Under the Back Porch" by Virginia Hamilton. Illustration copyright © 1992 by Pat Cummings.

Dial Books for Young Readers, a division of Penguin Books USA Inc.: "I Love the Look of Words" by Maya Angelou from *Soul Looks Back in Wonder* by Tom Feelings. Text copyright © 1993 by Maya Angelou; illustration copyright © 1993 Tom Feelings.

Doubleday, a division of Bantam Doubleday Dell Publishing Group, Inc.: "Two Horses," adapted from "The Riddle" in *Jewish Folktales* by Pinhas Sadeh. Text copyright © 1989 by Doubleday, a division of Bantam Doubleday Dell Publishing Group, Inc.

Dilys Evans Fine Illustration: Cover illustration by Lynne Dennis from *Shiloh* by Phyllis Reynolds Naylor. Illustration copyright © 1991 by Lynne Dennis.

Farrar, Straus & Giroux, Inc.: From *Whose Side Are You On?* by Emily Moore. Text copyright © 1988 by Emily Moore. Cover illustration by Peter Catalanotto from *The Green Book* by Jill Paton Walsh. Illustration copyright © 1986 by Peter Catalanotto.

Sheldon Fogelman, on behalf of Jerry Pinkney: Cover illustration by Jerry Pinkney from *Pride of Puerto Rico* by Paul Robert Walker. Copyright © 1988 by Harcourt Brace & Company.

Russell Freedman: From "Bring 'em Back Alive" by Russell Freedman in *The Story of Ourselves*, edited by Michael O. Tunnell and Richard Ammon. Text copyright © 1993 by Russell Freedman.

Greenwillow Books, a division of William Morrow & Company, Inc.: "The Line" and "Never Set Foot" from *Still More Stories to Solve: Fourteen Folktales from Around the World* by George Shannon, illustrated by Peter Sis. Text copyright © 1994 by George W. B. Shannon; illustrations copyright © 1994 by Peter Sis.

Hampton-Brown Books: "Dream America" by Juan Quintana, "What Flies Free" by Ina Cumpiano, and "The Outside/Inside Poem" by Sara Chan from *A Chorus of Cultures: Developing Literacy Through Multicultural Poetry* by Alma Flor Ada, Violet J. Harris, and Lee Bennett Hopkins. Text copyright © 1993 by Hampton-Brown Books.

Harcourt Brace & Company: From *The American Family Farm* by Joan Anderson, photographs by George Ancona. Text copyright © 1989 by Joan Anderson; photographs © 1989 by George Ancona. *Dear Benjamin Banneker* by Andrea Davis Pinkney, illustrated by Brian Pinkney. Text copyright © 1994 by Andrea Davis Pinkney; illustrations copyright © 1994 by Brian Pinkney. "Nickel-a-Pound Plane Ride" from *Local News* by Gary Soto. Text copyright © 1993 by Gary Soto.

HarperCollins Publishers: "Her Dreams" from *Under the Sunday Tree* by Eloise Greenfield, illustrated by Mr. Amos Ferguson. Text copyright © 1988 by Eloise Greenfield; illustrations copyright © 1988 by Amos Ferguson. From *Hector Lives in the United States Now* by Joan Hewett, photographs by Richard Hewett. Text copyright © 1990 by Joan Hewett; photographs copyright © 1990 by Richard R. Hewett. Untitled poem (Retitled: "Three Wishes") from *Near the Window Tree* by Karla Kuskin. Text copyright © 1975 by Karla Kuskin. Cover illustration by Marc Simont from *In the Year of the Boar and Jackie Robinson* by Bette Bao Lord. Illustration copyright © 1984 by Marc Simont. Cover illustration by Ruth Sanderson from *The Facts and Fictions of Minna Pratt* by Patricia MacLachlan. Illustration copyright © 1988 by Ruth Sanderson. Cover illustration by Marcia Sewall from *Sarah, Plain and Tall* by Patricia MacLachlan. Illustration copyright © 1985 by Marcia Sewall.

Holiday House, Inc.: Cover illustration by Terea Shaffer from *The Singing Man* by Angela Shelf Medearis. Illustration copyright © 1994 by Terea Shaffer.

Houghton Mifflin Company: From *Amish Home* by Raymond Bial. Copyright © 1993 by Raymond Bial.

Hyperion Books for Children: From *Morning Girl* by Michael Dorris. Text copyright © 1992 by Michael Dorris; cover illustration © 1992 By Kam Mak.

Alfred A. Knopf, Inc.: "April Rain Song" by Langston Hughes from *The Collected Poems of Langston Hughes*, edited by Arnold Rampersad. Text copyright © 1994 by the Estate of Langston Hughes.

Little, Brown and Company: From *Yang the Youngest and His Terrible Ear* by Lensey Namioka, illustrated by Kees de Kiefte. Text copyright © 1992 by Lensey Namioka; illustrations copyright © 1992 by Kees de Kiefte. Cover illustration by Kees de Kiefte from *Yang the Third and Her Impossible Family* by Lensey Namioka. Illustration copyright © 1995 by Kees de Kiefte.

Lodestar Books, an affiliate of Dutton Children's Books, a division of Penguin Books USA Inc.: From *Spanish Pioneers of the Southwest* by Joan Anderson, photographs by George Ancona. Text copyright © 1989 by Joan Anderson; photographs copyright © 1989 by George Ancona. Cover illustration by Pierre Bon from *Earth, Sky, and Beyond: A Journey Through Space* by Jean-Pierre Verdet, translated by Carol Volk. Copyright © 1993 by l'école des loisirs, Paris; English translation copyright © 1995 by Penguin Books USA Inc. Originally published in France by l'école des loisirs, 1993.

Lothrop, Lee & Shepard Books, a division of William Morrow & Company, Inc.: Cover photograph from *To Space & Back* by Sally Ride and Susan Okie. Copyright © 1986 by Sally Ride and Susan Okie. Cover illustration by Carole Byard from *Have a Happy...* by Mildred Pitts Walter. Illustration copyright © 1989 by Carole Byard.

Macmillan Publishing Company, a division of Macmillan, Inc.: Cover illustration by Eros Keith from *The House of Dies Drear* by Virginia Hamilton. Illustration copyright © 1968 by Eros Keith. Cover photograph by Christopher G. Knight from *Sugaring Time* by Kathryn Lasky. Photograph copyright © 1983 by Christopher G. Knight.

Claudia Cangilla McAdam: "Christopher Marshall: Up, Up, and Away" by Claudia Cangilla McAdam from *CRICKET* Magazine, April 1992. Text © 1992 by Claudia Cangilla McAdam.

Margaret K. McElderry Books, an imprint of Simon & Schuster: "Speak Up" from *Good Luck Gold and Other Poems* by Janet S. Wong. Text copyright © 1994 by Janet S. Wong.

McGraw-Hill Inc.: From book #60660 *The Log of Christopher Columbus* by Robert H. Fuson. Text copyright 1987 by Robert H. Fuson. Originally published by International Marine Publishing Company, Camden, ME.

Joseph T. Mendola Ltd., on behalf of Steve Brennan: Cover illustration by Steve Brennan from *A Gathering of Days* by Joan W. Blos. Illustration copyright © 1990 by Steve Brennan.

Francisco Mora: Cover illustration by Francisco Mora from *Local News* by Gary Soto. Published by Harcourt Brace & Company, 1993.

Morrow Junior Books, a division of William Morrow & Company, Inc.: From *Dear Mr. Henshaw* by Beverly Cleary, cover illustration by Paul O. Zelinsky. Text and illustration copyright © 1983 by Beverly Cleary. Cover illustration by Paul O. Zelinsky from *Strider* by Beverly Cleary. Illustration copyright © 1991 by William Morrow and Company, Inc. Cover illustration by Diane deGroat from *Aldo Peanut Butter* by Johanna Hurwitz. Illustration copyright © 1990 by Diane deGroat.

National Geographic Society Book Division: From "Appalachian Highlands" and maps by William H. Bond in *National Geographic Picture Atlas of Our Fifty States*. Copyright © 1991 by National Geographic Society.

Orchard Books, New York: Beethoven Lives Upstairs by Barbara Nichol, illustrated by Scott Cameron. Text copyright © 1993 by Classical Productions for Children Limited; illustrations copyright © 1993 by Scott Cameron.

Philomel Books: Illustrations by Robert Sabuda from *The Log of Christopher Columbus*, compiled by Steve Lowe. Illustrations copyright © 1992 by Robert Sabuda.

Plays, Inc.: Mary McLeod Bethune, Dream Maker by Mary Satchell from *Plays of Black Americans*, edited by Sylvia E. Kamerman. Text copyright © 1987 by Sylvia K. Burack. This play is for reading purposes only; for permission to produce, write to Plays, Inc., Publishers, 120 Boylston Street, Boston, MA 02116 USA.

Puffin Books, a division of Penguin Books USA Inc.: Cover illustration by Alan Olson from *Just My Luck* by Emily Moore. Illustration copyright © 1991 by Alan Olson.

G. P. Putnam's Sons: From *Homesick, My Own Story* by Jean Fritz, cover illustration by Margot Tomes. Text copyright © 1982 by Jean Fritz; cover illustration copyright © 1982 by Margot Tomes.

Roberts Rinehart Publishers: The People Who Hugged the Trees by Deborah Lee Rose, illustrated by Birgitta Säflund. Text copyright © 1990 by Deborah Lee Rose; illustrations copyright © 1990 by Birgitta Säflund.

Melodye Rosales: Cover illustration by Melodye Rosales from *Beetles, Lightly Toasted* by Phyllis Reynolds Naylor. Illustration copyright © 1987 by Melodye Rosales.

Scholastic Inc.: Cover illustration from *Good-Bye My Wishing Star* by Vicki Grove. Copyright © 1988 by Vicki Grove. From *Radio Fifth Grade* by Gordon Korman. Text and cover illustration copyright © 1989 by Gordon Korman. *By the Dawn's Early Light* by Steven Kroll, illustrated by Dan Andreasen. Text copyright © 1994 by Steven Kroll; illustrations copyright © 1994 by Dan Andreasen. Cover illustration by Elroy Freem from *...If You Traveled West in a Covered Wagon* by Ellen Levine. Illustration copyright © 1992 by Scholastic Inc.

Simon & Schuster Books for Young Readers, a division of Simon & Schuster: From *If You Were There in 1492* by Barbara Brenner. Copyright © 1991 by Barbara Brenner. From *A Very Young Musician* by Jill Krementz. Text copyright © 1991 by Jill Krementz. Cover illustration by Eileen McKeating from *After Fifth Grade, the World!* by Claudia Mills. Illustration copyright © 1989 by Eileen McKeating. From *Hatchet* by Gary Paulsen. Text copyright © 1987 by Gary Paulsen. "Night" from *The Collected Poems of Sara Teasdale*. Text copyright 1930 by Sara Teasdale Filsinger, renewed 1958 by Guaranty Trust Company of New York. Cover illustration by Pat Cummings from *Mariah Keeps Cool* by Mildred Pitts Walter. Illustration copyright © 1990 by Pat Cummings.

Smithmark Publishers, Inc.: Cover photograph by James Duncan from *Step-By-Step Paper Fun for Kids* by Marion Elliot. © 1994 by Anness Publishing Limited.

Ticknor & Fields Books for Young Readers, a Houghton Mifflin Company imprint: "Backwoods Scholars" from *A Pioneer Sampler* by Barbara Greenwood. Text copyright © 1994 by Barbara Greenwood.

Time, Inc.: "Golden Gate Bridge, World's Longest Span, Opens May 28" from *Life* Magazine, May 31, 1937. Text copyright 1937 by Time Inc.

United Press International: "Boy Pilot Resumes Historic Trans-Atlantic Crossing" by Warren Perley, July 11, 1988. Text copyright © 1988 by United Press International.

Viking Penguin, a division of Penguin Books USA Inc.: Cover illustration by Ted CoConis from *The Summer of the Swans* by Betsy Byars. Copyright © 1970 by Betsy Byars.

Neil Waldman: Cover illustration by Neil Waldman from *Hatchet* by Gary Paulsen. Illustration copyright © 1987 by Bradbury Press.

Franklin Watts: Cover photograph courtesy of the American Museum of Natural History from *North American Indian Survival Skills* by Karen Liptak. Copyright © 1990 by Karen Liptak.

Albert Whitman & Company: Cover illustration by James Watling from *Along the Santa Fe Trail: Marion Russell's Own Story* by Marion Russell, adapted by Ginger Wadsworth. Illustration copyright © 1993 by James Watling.

World Book Publishing: From "Flags in American History" in *The World Book Encyclopedia*, Volume 7. © 1992 by World Book, Inc.

Joyce Audy Zarins: Illustrations by Joyce Audy Zarins from "Patchwork Quilting" by Anita Howard Wade in *CRICKET* Magazine, September 1995.

Photo Credits

Key: (t) top, (b) bottom, (c) center, (l) left, (r) right.

Katherine Lambert, 106; Parallel Productions, 130; Ron Reeves, 151; Tom Sobolik/Black Star/Harcourt Brace & Company, 202, 341, 343, 365; George Ancona, 438-453,518-533; Terry Halsey/Black Star/Harcourt Brace & Company, 573; Albert Bierstadt, National Museum of American Art, Washington, D.C., Art Resource, NY, 513-522; Oscar E. Berninghaus, The Sid Richardson Collection of American Art, Fort Worth, 574; Bethune-Cookman College, 238-253, 256-257; The Colorado Historical Society, 541(t); Raymond Bial, 454-463, 466-467; The Denver Public Library, Wetern History Department,534-536, 547; Emanuel Gottlieb Leutze, The Metropolitan Museum of American Art, Gift of John S. Kennedy 1897, 158-159; Painting by Betsy Graves Reyeau, The Granger Collection, 246; Yvonne Jacquette, The Metropolitan Museum of Art, Purchase, Friends of the Department Gifts and matching funds from the National Endowment for the Arts, 1978, 258-259; The Maryland Historical Society,363;Jill Krementz, 388-403; The National Archives, 534(b); Pierre-Auguste Renoir, Mr. and Mrs. Martin A. Ryerson Collection, The Art Institute of Chicago, 369; Diego Rivera, University Art Museum, Berkeley, 468-469; Allan Rohan Crite, The National Museum of American Art, Washington, D.C., Art Resource, NY, 76-77; Scientific American/George V. Kelvin, 503-504(c); Stock Montage, Inc., 244;Mike Wilkins, The National Museum of American Art, Washington, D.C., Art Resource, NY, 204; Henry Wolf/The Image Bank, 240, 241, 245, 248, 249, 250, 251, 251, (borders)

Illustration Credits

Tom Lochray, Cover Art, Andrew Powell 22, 24-25, 29-32, 34-35, 39, 41, 43; Tom Feelings 46-47; David Coulson 50-55; Tyrone Geter 56-71; Pat Cummings 72-73; Michael Sours 78-87; Bob Dombrowski 88-107; Fabricio Vanden Broeck 118-131; George Littlefield 132-133; Robert Sabuda 136-151; Raphaelle Goethals 152-155; Margot Tomes 160-162, 164-168, 170-172; Darrin Johnston 176-179; Brian Pinkney 180-201; Navin Patel and Leanne M. Johnson 202-203; David Johnson 214-229; Tracy Sabin 234-235; Mr. Amos Ferguson 254; Darrin Johnston 255; Jacqueline Rogers 260-275; Lisa Palombo 276-277; Jennifer Hewitson 280-287; John Rosato 288-291, 293, 294, 296-299, 301, 302, 305, 307, 308, 310-311, 313-317; Sandra Shap 326-340, 342-343; Dan Andreasen 346-362, 364; Claudia Carlson 360 (map); Mary Lynn Blasutta 370-372, 374-378, 380-381, 383 (lettering); Kees de Kiefte 371, 373-376, 378, 380, 382; Scott Cameron 404-405, 407, 408, 411, 413, 414, 417, 418, 421, 423, 426-427, 429; Joyce Audy Zarins 464, 465; Birgitta Säflund 470-481; Hui Han Liu 482-483; Peter Sis 486-491; Tony Novak 508-509; Heidi King 434-35, 544-545 (lettering); Mercedes McDonald 548; Pamela Patrick 554-555, 557, 558, 560-561, 563-566, 568, 571, 572; Guy Porfirio 588-589